Ozumacín Chinantec Texts

Summer Institute of Linguistics
Language Data Amerindian Series

Publication 11

Folklore Texts in Mexican
Indian Languages 2

Nadine Rupp
Series Editor

Ozumacín Chinantec Texts

James E. Rupp and Nadine Rupp
Compilers

Marcial Méndez de la Cruz
Narrator

A Publication of
The Summer Institute of Linguistics
Dallas
1994

LANGUAGE DATA is a serial publication of the Summer Institute of Linguistics, Inc. The series is intended as an outlet for data-oriented papers authored by members of the Institute. All volumes are issued as microfiche editions, while certain selected volumes are also printed in off-set editions.

Copies of this and other publications of the Summer Institute of Linguistics may be obtained from

International Academic Bookstore
7500 W. Camp Wisdom Road
Dallas, TX 75236

Contents

Editor's Preface

This is the second volume in the series "Folklore Texts in Mexican Indian Languages" by the Summer Institute of Linguistics. The texts are accompanied by a short cultural sketch, a brief description of the phonemes, and information on the narrator.

The Indian language is presented in a phonemic transcription and each word has an English gloss. Free translations are given in Spanish and in English.

The publication of texts in this series combines the results of linguistic and anthropological research sponsored by the Summer Institute of Linguistics and makes available to the general public some valuable cultural material.

This volume of Ozumacín Chinantec texts follows the theme of creation and how life was in the beginning days after light appeared. "When Loads Moved Themselves along the Trail" tells of when the world was new and people did not have to carry their possessions. They simply spoke their command and the load began to roll along the trail in front of the owner. "When Light Came to the Earth" tells of the creatures that existed and how some became various animals known today and how some became people. "A Brother and Sister Become the Sun and the Moon" relates the adventures of a brother and sister who set out looking for work. After they encounter danger and experience delays they finally are given the responsibility of being the sun and the moon. A hired hand, in the next tale, exchanges the King's bull for a wife and is afraid to tell the King; but the story has a happy ending. In "A Rabbit Who Buys a Guitar," the rabbit finds some money and buys a guitar. He plays it for the other animals and almost loses it to the skunk. "The Opossum and the Coyote" tells of how each one tries to trick the other over and over. "About Beings who Live in the River" tells of how children splashing in the water disturb the water beings and of the consequences to the family.

My husband, Jim Rupp, and I began field work in the Ozumacín Chinantec language in 1984 and continue study to the present.

Nadine Rupp
Editor

Introduction

Cultural Sketch of the Ozumacín Chinantecs

Speakers of the Ozumacín Chinantec language live in three major villages, Ayotzintepec, Ozumacín, and Santiago Progreso, all located in the northeast area of the state of Oaxaca. They are less than 100 miles from the Veracruz coast and lie in the low tropical areas at the foot of the Eastern Sierra Madre. In relation to the Chinantla (area of twelve distinct Chinantec languages), this language group is located in the south central area.

Approximately 5,000 people speak this language, many of whom also speak Spanish to a limited degree. However, there are some who have little or no knowledge of Spanish, especially among the older women. Chinantec is spoken in all the homes, and the children learn it first. While they recognize Spanish as the prestigious language, their own language is valued highly.

The climate is hot and humid with an abundance of yearly rainfall that results in rivers and streams throughout the area. The lush vegetation is typical of tropical areas with palm, mango, banana, and orange trees being the most prominent.

Two crops a year are harvested because of the long, warm growing season and the abundance of rain. Corn is the main staple for their sustenance, with chili peppers being their main cash crop. They grow enough coffee for their own use and market small amounts. Sugar cane is widely cultivated and men often leave the villages to go to the larger sugar cane fields for temporary work during harvest time. Domesticated animals include dogs, chickens, ducks, turkeys, horses, and cows.

1

The federal school system has built facilities and provides Spanish-speaking teachers in all three towns. The majority of the children attend school and go through a minimum of six grades. Young people are increasingly going to bigger towns to get more education.

With the arrival of roads and electricity, influences from the national culture stand sharply in contrast to the culture as it existed for many years. Concrete block houses with tin or aluminum roofs are quickly replacing the traditional stick and thatch palm houses. However, those who have the block houses still have a kitchen made with a thatch palm roof for their open-fire cooking. Electricity has brought things like blenders, refrigerators, and in a few cases, television sets and video cassette recorders. Most homes have a radio, an audio cassette player, and several members of the household might own watches.

The common diet consists of corn tortillas, eggs, beans, chili peppers, some vegetables, coffee, and fruits such as oranges, a variety of bananas, avocados, and coconuts. A centrally-located mill for grinding corn relieves households of the task of grinding corn by hand.

Although Chinantecs in general are noted for their beautiful and intricate weavings, especially huipiles, the Ozumacín Chinantecs seem to have lost this art. They have adopted the typical western look in their dress.

Narrator

Marcial Méndez de la Cruz, a native speaker of Ozumacín Chinantec, wrote these stories out on paper after he learned to read and write his own language. Because he did not yet have total control of some aspects of writing and spelling, some editing has occurred. He wrote a total of eighty-four stories, including first-hand experiences, local historical events, stories he heard from the older generation, procedural instructions, hortatory discourses, and prayers. These were all recorded during the period of 1986–1989.

Brief description of Ozumacín phonemes

Following is a phonemic transcription of all phonemes in the language.

Vowels. There are ten vowels; *i, e, a, o, u, ï, ë, ä, ö, ü*. Each of these may be nasalized, which is indicated by a Polish hook under the vowel. Nasalization is often associated with animate gender, but there are inanimate nouns that are nasalized. Vowel length is contrastive and is indicated by a colon following the vowel.

Consonants. The inventory of consonants in Chinantec are: *p, t, k, b, d, g, ?, č, z* (representing *dz*), *ǰ, s, h, m, n, ñ, ŋ, l,* and *r.*

Palatalization. In the verb paradigms there are two basic patterns of palatalization: one affects only the intentive aspect of every person; and another, which is more prominent, where every aspect of first person plural is palatalized along with the completive aspect of second person.

When the initial consonant is *k, g, t, l,* or *n,* the palatalization is realized as vowel fronting. For example *ë* becomes *e, ï* becomes *i.* When the consonant is *t, l,* or *n* the vowels that are affected are usually *a, o,* and *u* and they become *ä, ö,* and *ü* respectively. An alternative analysis might be to represent these three vowels as /ia/, /io/, and /iu/ so that Ozumacín would then have only seven vowels and thus more closely match the number of vowels in other Chinantec languages. However, for this presentation we have chosen to speak of ten vowels, which represent the surface phenomena, rather than the more abstract symbolization which implies a vowel glide. In other Chinantec languages the palatalization is retained on the surface as a transition sound.

When palatalization involves the consonants *s, z,* and *ŋ,* normally both the consonant and the vowel are affected. The consonants each move to the alveopalatal point of articulation, becoming: *č, ǰ,* and *ñ* respectively. The vowel is palatalized (fronted) except when the vowel is *a* or *o* which remain unchanged. Again, a more abstract analysis would treat these consonants as *si, zi,* and *ŋi,* but it does not then represent contemporary Ozumacín Chinantec, except perhaps for *ŋi.*

Another kind of consonant cluster involves *k, g, ?,* and *h.* Both *i* and *u* combine with each before certain nuclear vowels. The front vowel [i] with one of these consonants precedes the vowels *e, a, o, u* and the back vowel [u] precedes *a, e, ë, ï, ä, o.*

Tone. There are three level tones, with a ballistic counterpart (which is realized phonetically as a rapid falling pitch) and a rising counterpart of each. The ballistic stress is written with an accent over the nuclear vowel. Tone is indicated at the end of each syllable with the following symbols: high tone ([H]), mid tone ([M]), low tone ([L]), high rising tone ([HR]), mid rising tone ([MR]), and low rising tone ([LR]).

Syllables. All Ozumacín Chinantec syllables are open or end in glottal stop, except when the clitic pronouns (/=n/, /=ʔ/, /=y/) are added.

Consonant clusters, which only occur syllable initially, are glottal stop or fricative followed by sonorant, specifically: ʔl, ʔm, ʔn, ʔŋ, hl, hm, hn, and hŋ.

Stress. Stress is only minimally important as a slight amplitude difference between stressed and unstressed syllables. Stress occurs on the stem of the word; stems are almost always monosyllabic. We suspect that each root in a compound gets equal stress, but have not studied this in detail. Since stress is predictable it is not indicated in the texts. Note that this phonetic stress is distinct from the ballistic or controlled contrast, which could be treated as a type of stress or accent.

Loan words. Spanish loan words are indicated with brackets (< >).

Clitics. The clitic pronouns n (first person), ʔ (second person), and y (third person) are separated from the stem and are shown as /=n/, /=ʔ/, /=y/.

Gloss. Certain particles which denote a particular grammatical function are abbreviated in the gloss line as follows: $če^M$ interrogative (?); ba^M emphasis (EMP); he: locative (LOC); $hạ^L$ deictic functioning as pause (PAUSE); na^L deictic functioning as pause (PAUSE); da^M direct discourse word (DDM); meaning uncertain or redundant.

When Loads Moved Themselves
along the Trail

1. *lá^{L}ma^{M}ʔmë́^{M} hmɨ́:^{L}gṹ:^{L} lá^{L}ma^{M}to^{L}gá^{L}nő:^{H} hmɨ́:^{L}gṹ:^{L} sá^L*
   when^was^new world   when^began   world   not

   ma^{M}hë̈:^{MR} za^L uɨ́:^{M}
   used^to^see people difficulty

2. *ʔñɨ́:^{M} ba^M d^{y}o^{HR} ma^{M}k^{w}á̧^{L} ʔe^L ku:ʔ^L za^L*
   himself (EMP) God used^to^give what were^eating people

3. *sá^L ča^L ʔe^L ʔlï:ʔ^H ma^{M}ča^L*
   not was what evil   used^to^be

4. *sá^L ča^L hu:^{H} k^{w}ạ:ʔ^H ma^{M}ča^L*
   not was word lewd   used^to^be

---

1. When the world was new,
   when the world began, people
   had no difficulty.

2. God himself provided food for
   people.

3. There was no evil.

4. There was no lewd talk.

1. Cuando el mundo era nuevo,
   cuando el mundo empezó, la
   gente no tenía problemas.

2. El mismo Dios proveía la
   comida para la gente.

3. No había maldad.

4. No había plática grosera.

5. $sá^L$ $ča^L$ $lë:^{LR}$ $ma^M ča^L$
not were jokes used^to^be

6. <pero> $ma^M gá^L lá^L h^w \acute{\underset{.}{e}}:^M$ za^L $gá^L lá^L h^w \acute{\underset{.}{e}}:^M$ $g\underset{.}{\ddot{u}}:^L$
but   when^became^many   people   became^many   children

$mó^L só^L$ $gá^L hmé:^M$ $či:?^L$ $g\underset{.}{\ddot{u}}:^L$ $?e^H$ $n\ddot{u}:?^{HR}$ $kí?^H$
no^longer they^did   children children attention advice of

za^L $ma^L k\underset{.}{a}:?^M$
people   now^big

7. $mó^L só^L$ $gá^L ?\ddot{\underset{.}{o}}:^M$ $či:?^L$ <respeto>
no^longer had   children respect

8. $gá^L hmé:^M$ $=i$ $l\acute{\underset{.}{a}}^H$ $?nö:$ $=i$ $?\tilde{n}í:^M$ $=i$ ba^M
did   they like wanted they themselves they (EMP)

9. <pero> $l\acute{\underset{.}{a}}^L ž\acute{u}^H$ $?e^L$ $sá^L$ $gá^L hmé:^M$ $=i$ $?e^H$ $?e^L$ $h\acute{\underset{.}{a}}?^M$
but   since   that not did   they attention what said

za^L $ma^L k\underset{.}{a}:?^M$ $?e^L$ $h\acute{\underset{.}{a}}?^M$ za^L $l\acute{\underset{.}{a}}^L$ la^L
people   now^big   that said   people like this

5. There were no jokes.

6. But when people multiplied, babies multiplied, the kids no longer paid attention to the advice of the adults.

7. Children no longer had respect.

8. They did what they wanted to.

9. But since they didn't pay attention to what the adults said, that people said like this:

5. No había chistes.

6. Pero cuando se multiplicó la gente, se multiplicaron los bebés, los muchachos dejaron de prestar atención al consejo de los adultos.

7. Ya no tenían respeto los niños.

8. Hacían lo que querían.

9. Pero siendo que no prestaban atención a lo que los adultos decían, esa gente dijo así:

10. *ua^Mráʔ^M ʔa^L ma^Lda^HR gá^Lžó:^M =ʔ tá^L ua^Mža^Mhę̃:^M =ʔ*
when where errand go you don't be^staring you

11. *tá^L hę̃:^L za^L ʔį:^L tä̧:ʔ^M kíʔ^H*
don't look^at people who are place

12. *tá^L ką^L k^wąta^MR kíʔ^H za^L*
don't take account to people

13. *tá^L hę̃:^M ʔe^L hmé:^L za^L*
don't look what are^doing people

14. *sá^L žú^H hną̃^M*
not good appears

15. *hą̧^L to:^L ʔǫ̧:^L na^L ba^M na^Lhlą̧:^HR ŋë^L =ʔ*
not hole grave (PAUSE) EMP uncovered walk you

10. "Wherever you go on an errand, don't be staring,

11. don't look at people where they are,

12. don't be examining people,

13. don't look at what people are doing.

14. It doesn't look good.

15. Don't walk around (with your mouth) like an open grave."

10. —Cuando vayas a un mandado, no te quedes examinando (a la gente),

11. no mires hacia donde está la gente,

12. no estés examinando a la gente,

13. no mires lo que la gente está haciendo.

14. No se ve bien.

15. No andes (con la boca) como una tumba abierta.

16. *lá^{L}žú^H ʔe^L sá^L gá^{L}ʔǿ^M či:ʔ^L lá^{L}hę́^{L} ʔe^L la^L*
    since   that not keep   children everything that here

   gá^{L}hą̃^{M} =i ʔlï:ʔ^H
   turned^out they evil

17. *kọ:^{L} ʔä^M gá^{L}nä́:^{H} ú:^{H} či:ʔ^L gá^{L}kị́:^{L} k^{w}ï:^{L}*
    one time went   two children brought^home corn

18. *ma^{L}tę́:^{M} =i tǫ́^{H}za:ʔ^{LR} h^{w}ë^H*
    reached they halfway road

19. *he:^{M} hą^L k^{y}e:^{L} kọ:^{L} hmï:^{L}*
    (LOC) there was a   river

20. *ʔñí:^{M} he:^{M} hą^L gá^{L}hę:^{H} =i kọ:^{L} lö:^{H} hóʔ^H*
    itself (LOC) there met   they a   load coming^home

21. *kę́:^{L} ga^M mi:ʔ^L za^L hü:^{M} lö:^{H} hą^L*
    behind more little person owner load (PAUSE)

22. *gá^{L}tạ:ʔ^{LR} či:ʔ^L ʔê^M tá^L kó:^{M}*
    stood   children those toward side

---

16. Since the kids didn't keep this (advice) here, it turned out bad for them.

16. Siendo que los muchachos no siguieron este consejo, resultó mal para ellos.

17. Once two boys went to bring in corn.

17. Una vez dos niños fueron a traer mazorcas.

18. They reached the halfway point.

18. Llegaron a medio camino.

19. There was a river.

19. Allá había un río.

20. Right there they met a load coming home.

20. Allá mismo encontraron una carga viniendo a su casa.

21. A little behind (came) the owner of the load.

21. Un poquito atrás (venía) el dueño de la carga.

22. The kids stood to one side.

22. Los niños se pararon a un lado.

23. *na:^{HR} ?e^L gá^{L}lá^H kí?^{H} lö:^{H} ha^L*
where what happened to load (PAUSE)

24. *ha^L gá^{L}ŋí:^{H} či:?^{L} ?é^M*
then laughed children those

25. *ha^L tä:?^{M} či:?^{L} ?é^M ŋï:^{MR} ma^{M}há?^{H} za^L*
then stood children those laughing when^came^home person

hü:^{M}
owner

26. *lá^{L}gá^{L}há^M ha^L ba^M lö:^{H} ha^L gá^{L}há^M ó^L?í?^{L}*
stayed there (EMP) load that was embarrassed

27. *ha^L ba^M čé?^{H} za^L ?é^M kï:^{L} bä^{MR} =i lö:^{H}*
then (EMP) was^standing person that rolling writhing he load

kí?^{H} =i ha^L
of him (PAUSE)

28. *gá^{L}ŋé^M ba^M či:?^{L} ?é^M h$^{wë H}$ gá^{L}ná:^{H} =i*
walked (EMP) children those way went they

23. Who knows what happened to the load!

24. Then those kids laughed.

25. There stood those kids laughing when the owner came.

26. The load just stayed right where it was, (it) was embarrassed.

27. That man kept standing there trying to move his load somehow.

28. The kids went on their way.

23. ¡Quién sabe qué le pasó a la carga!

24. Entonces esos niños se rieron.

25. Allí estaban esos niños parados, riéndose, cuando vino el dueño.

26. La carga sólo se quedó allá, donde estaba; estaba apenada.

27. Ese hombre se quedó parado allá, tratando de mover su carga de alguna manera.

28. Los niños siguieron su camino.

29. *gá^{L}lá^{L}mé:ʔ^L zẽ^H* *zal* *ʔé^M sá^L ʔi:^{MR} ŋẽ^H lö:^{H} ha^L*
    got^sad heart person that not agreed walk load (PAUSE)

30. *ha^L ga^M gá^{L}ká^H =i lö:^{H} kíʔ^H =i h^{w}ẽ^M ka^{M}lu:^{M} =i*
    then more carried he load of him road back his

31. *ma^{M}gá^{L}žá^{L}nã:^{H} či:ʔ^L ʔé^M móʔ^M kíʔ^H =i gá^{L}hmé:^{M} =i*
    when^arrived children those ranch of them prepared they

    lö:^{H} kíʔ^H =i
    load of them

32. *ma^{M}gá^{L}lá^H lö:^{H} kíʔ^H =i ha^L hãʔ^M =i sí:ʔ^L =i*
    when^were^ready load of them then said they told they

    lö:^{H} kíʔ^H =i ma:^{LR} hni^M ha^L
    load of them let's^go we (PAUSE)

33. *ní^L sá^L gá^{L}héʔ^H lö:^{H} ha^L he:^{M} k^{y}e:^{L}*
    even not move load (PAUSE) (LOC) were

29. That man became sad, the load refused to go.

30. Finally he carried his load on his back.

31. When the kids arrived at their ranch, they prepared their loads.

32. When their loads were ready, they said to their loads: "Let's go."

33. The loads didn't even move where they lay.

29. Ese hombre se entristeció, la carga no quiso caminar.

30. Finalmente, él llevó su carga en la espalda.

31. Cuando los niños llegaron a su rancho, prepararon sus cargas.

32. Cuando estuvieron listas sus cargas, le dijeron a sus cargas: —Vamos.

33. Las cargas ni siquiera se movieron de donde estaban.

34. $sá^L$ $zá^{M\wedge}zë^H$ $=i$ $ʔe^L$ $gá^Lŋí:^H$ $=i$ $kíʔ^H$ $lö:^H$ $kíʔ^H$ $za^Lk^yạ:ʔ^M$
    not recall   they what laughed they at   load of   companion

    $=i$
    their

35. $ʔe^Lhạ^L$ $hạ^L$ $kạ^{MR}$ $=i$ $lö:^H$ $ka^Mlu:^M$ $=i$ $lá^Lhị:ʔ^L$ $ná^H$
    thus   then carry they load back   their until   now

34. They didn't recall that they had laughed at the load of their companion.

35. That's why (people) carry loads on their backs to this day.

34. Ellos no recordaron que se habían reído de la carga de su compañero.

35. Es por eso que la (gente) lleva su carga en la espalda hasta hoy.

When Light Came to the Earth

1. *lá̤^{L} la^L lá^H ko̤:^{L}* <*cuento*> *Ɂe^L žá^L za^L ma^{L}g^{y}ṳ:Ɂ^L*
   like this is a story what tell people old

2. *lá̤^{L} la^L ba^M ma^{M}lá^H žó:^{M}hó:^{H} ko^{L}te^{MR} lá̤:^{M} =i*
   like this (EMP) used^to^be long^time^ago very thought they

3. *lá̤^{L}ma^{M}Ɂmë̤:^{M} hmí:^{L}gṳ:^{L} lá̤^{L}hë́^{L} hmï:^{M} ba^M lá^H lá̤^{L} lá^H Ɂe^L*
   when^was^new world every day (EMP) was like was that

   ma^{L}zá^H Ɂ^{y}o̤:^{L}
   ran^out sun

4. *sá^L hnä̤^{M} hë̤:^{L}*
   not appear clear

1. This is a story that the old people tell.	1. Ésta es una historia que los viejos cuentan.
2. This is how it used to be a long time ago, they thought.	2. Ellos piensan que así fue hace mucho tiempo.
3. When the world was new, each day it was as if the sun had run out.	3. Cuando el mundo era nuevo, cada día era como si el sol se hubiera acabado.
4. It was not clear.	4. No estaba claro.

5. *kọ:^{L}*   *ma^{M}gá^{L}lá^{L}čá^L*   *hu:^{H}*   *há?^{M}*   *za^L*   *ų́:?^{L}*
    all^of^a^sudden   when^was   story   said   people   will^cross

    në^M   *hni^M*
    upon   us

6. *gá^{L}h^{w}ạ:?^{H}*   *h^{w}ërte za^L*   *?é^M*
    were^frightened very   people those

7. *<pero>*   *za^L*   *?é^M*   *ma^{M}lạ́:^{H}*   *=i*   *kạ́:?^{M}*   *ba^M*
    but   people those used^to^be they   different   (EMP)

8. *sá^L*   *ča^L*   *?mï:?^{L}*   *kí?^{H}*   *=i*   *ma^{M}ča^L*
    not was clothes of   them were

9. *?ị:^{L}*   *ma^{M}gá^{L}nä:^{M}*   *tó^{L}ló^{L}k^{w}ạ́:?^{L}* *ba^M*   *?é^M*
    who used^to^go^around naked   (EMP) those

10. *sá^L* *ma^{M}lạ́:^{H}*   *=i*   *lá^L*   *lạ́:^{H}* *za^L*   *čạ:^{L}*   *ná^H*
    not used^to^be they like are people there^are now

5. Suddenly there was a report, people said, "Let's cross ourselves."

5. De pronto, hubo un estallido, y dijo la gente: —Vamos a cruzar nosotros.

6. Those people were very afraid.

6. Esa gente tenía mucho miedo.

7. Now those people were different.

7. Bueno, esa gente era diferente.

8. They didn't have clothes.

8. No tenían ropa.

9. They used to go around naked rather.

9. Ellos más bien andaban desnudos.

10. They were not like the people who live now.

10. No eran como la gente que vive ahora.

11. *he·ᴹ gáᴸnä·ᴹ =i ʔno·ᴸ =i ʔeᴸ ku·ʔᴸ =i*
(LOC) go^around they looking^for they what were^eating they

kǫ·ᴸ maᴹháᴴ hmé·ᴸ gáᴸláᴸhnäᴹ
all^of^a^sudden when^came does appeared

12. *háᴴ gáᴸhę̈·ᴹ láᴴ*
came cleared was

13. *gáᴸtǫ́·ᴹ gü·ʔᴴ*
became^white sky

14. *hą̈ᴸ gáᴸtą·ʔᴸᴿ =i hë·ᴸᴿ zą́ʔᴸ =i*
then stood they were^looking amazed they

15. *kǫ·ᴸ maᴹgáᴸtą́·ʔᴴ hmę̈·ᴴ ʔʸo·ᴸ néʔᴸ nu·ᴸ*
all^of^a^sudden when^entered light sun into woods

16. *hą̈ᴸ gáᴸhʷą·ʔᴸᴿ =i hʷërte*
then were^frightened they very

17. *hą̈ᴸ gáᴸtą·ʔᴸᴿ =i hë·ᴸᴿ =i ʔeᴸ naᴸ*
then stood they were^looking they what that

11. While they went around looking for food, suddenly it became visible.

12. It cleared up;

13. the sky became white.

14. They stood amazed.

15. Suddenly the sunlight entered the woods.

16. And they were really afraid.

17. Thus they stood staring at it.

11. Mientras iban a buscar comida, de pronto se pudo ver.

12. Se aclaró;

13. los cielos se volvieron blancos.

14. Ellos se detuvieron asombrados.

15. De pronto, la luz del sol penetró en el bosque.

16. Y se asustaron mucho.

17. Así que, se quedaron mirándolo.

18. $ko:^L$ $ma^Mgá^Llá^Lhnǎ^M$ $\gamma o:^L$ $në^M$ $mó\gamma^M$
    all^of^a^sudden when^appeared sun   upon mountain

19. $hi:\gamma^H$ $g^y\acute{e}:\gamma^M$ $lá^L$ $hmé:^L$ $há^H$
    shiny bright like was^making came

20. $<pero>$ $ma^Mgá^Lhé:^H$ $=i$ $k^we:^L$ $sá^L$ $tá:^M{}^na^L$ $=i$
    but   when^saw   they carefully not tarry   they

21. $gá^Lk^y\acute{u}:^H$ $=i$
    ran   they

22. $gá^Lta:\gamma^{LR}$ $\gamma i:^L$ $gá^Lta:\gamma^{LR}$ $né\gamma^L$ $to:^L$ $\gamma^wá^H$
    stood   who stood   into hole ground

23. $\gamma i:^L$ $\gamma é^M$ $gá^Llé:^H$ $hü:\gamma^M$
    who those became armadillos

24. $gá^Lta:\gamma^{LR}$ $\gamma i:^L$ $gá^Lta:\gamma^{LR}$ $né\gamma^L$ $to:^L$ γma^L $né\gamma^L$ $to:^L$ $ku:^M$
    stood   who stood   into hole tree into hole rock

18. Suddenly the sun appeared on the mountain.

19. It was very bright and shiny in coming.

20. But when they looked carefully, they did not tarry;

21. they fled.

22. Some entered holes in the ground.

23. These became armadillos.

24. Some entered into holes in the trees, and into holes in rocks.

18. De pronto, el sol apareció sobre las montañas.

19. Estaba muy brillante y deslumbrante al salir.

20. Pero cuando miraron con cuidado, no se detuvieron;

21. ellos corrieron.

22. Algunos se metieron en hoyos (que había) en la tierra.

23. Éstos se convirtieron en armadillos.

24. Algunos se metieron dentro de los hoyos de los árboles y de las rocas.

25. *ʔį·ᴸ ʔéᴹ gáᴸlę́·ᴴ ŋaᴹ*
    who those became spotted^cavy

26. *gáᴸlę́·ᴹ ñéᴴ^nu·ᴸ*
    became wild^peccary

27. *gáᴸuį́·ᴴ ʔį·ᴸ gáᴸuį́·ᴴ gü·ʔᴴ*
    climbed who climbed up

28. *ʔį·ᴸ ʔéᴹ gáᴸlę́·ᴴ kʸéᴴ*
    who those became coatimundis

29. *ʔį·ᴸ ʔéᴹ gáᴸlę́·ᴴ maᴸčę·ᴸᴿ*
    who those became monkeys

30. *gáᴸʔmä·ʔᴸ ʔį·ᴸ gáᴸʔmä·ʔᴸ he·ᴹ nu·ᴸ*
    hid   who hid   (LOC) woods

31. *ʔį·ᴸ ʔéᴹ gáᴸlę́·ᴴ čų̈·ᴹ*
    who those became brocket^deer

32. *koᴸžą·ᴹ ʔį·ᴸ ʔʷe·ʔᴸ^zę́ᴴ ʔį·ᴸ tä̈ʔᴹ he·ᴹ hʷį·ᴸ sáᴸ gáᴸkʸų̈·ᴴ*
    some who brave   who were (LOC) town not flee

25. These became spotted cavies

26. and wild peccaries.

27. Some went up (in trees).

28. They became coatimundis,

29. and those became monkeys.

30. Some hid in the woods.

31. These became brocket deer.

32. Those who were brave who were in the town, they didn't flee.

25. Éstos se convirtieron en agutíes

26. y jabalíes.

27. Algunos se treparon (a los árboles).

28. Se convirtieron en coatíes,

29. y ésos se convirtieron en monos.

30. Algunos se escondieron en el bosque.

31. Éstos se convirtieron en gamos.

32. Los que fueron valientes que se quedaron en el pueblo, no corrieron.

33. *ʔi̧:ᴸ ʔéᴹ gáᴸláᴴ žú̧ᴴ kiʔᴴ*
    who those happened well for^them

34. *gáᴸhȩ́:ᴴ =i ʔʸo:ᴸ*
    looked they sun

35. *gáᴸŋȩ́ᴹ =i he:ᴹ hnã̧ᴹ ʔʸo:ᴸ*
    walked they (LOC) appears sun

36. *gáᴸlá̧ᴸsi̧:ᴴ móᴸsóᴸ láᴴ lá̧ᴸ maᴹlá̧ᴴ*
    changed no^longer was like used^to^be

37. *gáᴸlá̧ᴸhná̧ᴹ si̧:ʔᴸ kaᴸlá̧ʔᴹ gáᴸlá̧ᴸhná̧ᴹ nú̧:ᴹ*
    appeared moon also appeared stars

38. *<i> móᴸsóᴸ gáᴸku:ʔᴸ =i <cosa> hʷí̧ʔᴴ lá̧ᴸ maᴹku:ʔᴸ*
    and no^longer ate they things raw like used^to^eat

    =i há̧:ᴴ
    they earlier

39. *gáᴸhnó̧:ʔᴴ =i heᴸ*
    discovered they fire

---

33. It turned out well for them.

33. A ellos les resultó bien.

34. They looked at the sun;

34. Miraron al sol;

35. they walked where the sun shone.

35. caminaron hacia donde el sol brillaba.

36. Things changed, no longer was it like it used to be.

36. Las cosas cambiaron, y ya no era como antes.

37. The moon could be seen also, the stars could be seen.

37. La luna se podía ver también, se podían ver las estrellas.

38. And they no longer ate things raw like they used to eat formerly.

38. Y ya no comían cosas crudas como acostumbraban antes.

39. They discovered fire.

39. Descubrieron el fuego.

40. *gá^{L}ku:ʔ^L* =*i* <*cosa*> *na^{L}k^{w}ï:^{H}*
    ate   they things   cooked

41. *mó^{L}só^L*   *lá^H kíʔ^H* =*i*   *lá̧^{L} ma^{M}lá^H*   *kíʔ^H* =*i*   *há̧·^{H}*
    no^longer was of   them like used^to^be of   them earlier

42. *gá^{L}ná̧^{M} ʔü:^{M}zȩ̈^{L} kíʔ^H* =*i*
    opened thought of   them

43. *gá^{L}lá̧^{L}hná̧^{M} hȩ̈·^{L}*   *lá̧^{L}ka̧:^{L} lá̧^{L}hú:ʔ^H hmḯ·^{L}gú:^{L}*
    appeared   clear all   totality world

44. *ʔlï:ʔ^H ko^{L}te^{MR} ba^M*   *ma^{M}lá^H*   *kíʔ^H za^L*   *g^{w}a̧·^{H}*
    bad   very   (EMP) used^to^be for   people old

45. *ma^{M}ku:ʔ^L*   =*i*   <*cosa*>   *h^{w}ḯʔ^H*
    used^to^eat they things   raw

46. *lá̧^{L} ha̧^{L} ba^M*   *ma^{M}lá^H*
    like that (EMP) used^to^be

47. *ní^H háʔ^M*   *sá^L ma^{M}góʔ^L*   *ka^{L}lá̧ʔ^M*
    nor animals not used^to^be^afraid also

40. They ate things that were cooked.

41. Things were no longer like it used to be formerly.

42. Their thinking was opened up.

43. The entire world was now seen clearly.

44. It used to be very bad for the ancient people;

45. they used to eat things raw.

46. That is how it used to be.

47. The animals did not used to be afraid.

40. Ellos comieron cosas cocidas.

41. Ya no era como había sido antes.

42. Se les abrió el pensamiento.

43. Todo el mundo se veía con claridad.

44. Era todo muy difícil (mal) para la gente antigua;

45. comían cosas crudas.

46. Así es como era antes.

47. Los animales no tenían miedo.

48. *kʸa̱:ʔᴹ ʔmaᴸ kʸa̱:ʔᴹ ku̱:ᴹ baᴹ maᴹhŋé̱:ʔᴸ zaᴸ há ʔᴹ*
   with   sticks with   rocks (EMP) used^to^kill people animals

49. *lá̱ᴸ ha̱ᴸ baᴹ gá ᴸlá́ᴴ   lá̱ᴸmaᴹʔmé̱:ᴹ hmí̱:ᴸgú̱:ᴸ*
   like that (EMP) happened when^was^new world

50. *ʔi̱:ᴸ ñeᴸ   čeᴹ zó:ᴹ*
   who knows if   true

51. *há ʔᴹ gá ʔᴹ zaᴸ   sáᴸ zó:ᴹ*
   say   some people not true

48. With sticks and with stones people killed animals.

49. This is how it happened when the world was new.

50. Who knows if it is true.

51. Some people say it is not true.

48. Con palos y piedras mataba la gente a los animales.

49. Eso es lo que sucedió cuando el mundo era nuevo.

50. ¡Quién sabe si es verdad!

51. Algunas personas dicen que no es verdad.

A Brother and Sister Become the Sun and the Moon

1. $\acute{u}$:^{H} za^L $ma^Lg^y\mu$:$\mathit{?}^L$ $g\acute{a}^L n\ddot{a}$:^{M} $m\acute{o}\mathit{?}^M$ $hm\acute{e}$:^{L} $=i$ ta^M
   two people old   used^to^go ranch were^doing they work

   $k\acute{\iota}\mathit{?}^H$ $=i$
   of   them

2. $\mathit{?}\underset{\sim}{a}$:^{MR} $=i$ $k\underset{\sim}{o}$:^{L} $hm\ddot{\imath}$:^{L} $h\underset{\sim}{a}^L$ ga^M $t\underset{\sim}{\acute{e}}$:^{H} $=i$ $m\acute{o}\mathit{?}^M$
   would^ford they a   river   then more would^reach they ranch

   $k\acute{\iota}\mathit{?}^H$ $=i$
   of   them

1. Two old people used to go to work at their ranch.

2. They would ford a river and then they would reach their ranch.

1. Dos viejecitos acostumbraban ir a trabajar a su rancho.

2. Tenían que cruzar un río para llegar a su rancho.

3. *ma^Mgá^Ltę́·^M* = *i* *ča^MPo·^M hmï·^L he·^M hạ^M gá^Lhę́·^H* = *i*
   when^reached they edge   river (LOC) there saw   they

   tä:P^M tǫ́^H mï̈^Hhlï:^L néP^L nu·^L pi:P^H
   were two eggs   in   grass short

4. *hạ^L gá^Lkǫ·^H* = *i gá^Llǫ́·^M* = *i Pmï:P^L*
   then carried they wrapped they cloth

5. *ma^Miá^Lnä·^LR* = *i ča^MnéP^L kíP^H* = *i hạ^L gá^Lkǫ·^H* = *i hlï·^L*
   when^returned they inside   place their then took   they eggs

   kíP^H = *i*
   of   them

6. *gá^Lto:P^L* = *i néP^L mï̈^Hk^wa:P^L lą́^L hạ^L lá^H <costumbre> kíP^H*
   put^in   they under bowl   like that is   custom   of

   = *i*
   them

7. *he·^M hạ^L to:P^L za^L hlï·^L kíP^H za^L čạ·^L*
   (LOC) there place people eggs of^them people there^are

   ča:P^M kíP^H
   chicken of^them

3. When they reached the river's edge, there they saw two eggs in the short grass.

4. They took them and wrapped them in a cloth.

5. When they arrived at their house, they took their eggs;

6. they put them in a squash bowl like their custom is.

7. That is where people put their eggs, those people who have chickens.

3. Cuando llegaron a la orilla del río vieron dos huevos en el pasto corto.

4. Los tomaron y los envolvieron en una tela.

5. Entonces ellos llegaron a su casa, tomaron los huevos,

6. los pusieron en un tazón, como es la costumbre.

7. Allá es donde la gente guarda los huevos; la gente que tiene gallinas.

8. *hą^L gá^Lto:ʔ^L =i kíʔ^H =i néʔ^L kʷa:ʔ^L*
   then put^in   they of   them under bowl

9. *gá^Lnä:^M bíʔ^H kíʔ^H =i*
   went   they place their

10. *gá^Lʔia^L mi:ʔ^L hmï:^M tä:ʔ^M hlï:^L kíʔ^H =i   ma^Mgá^Llô:^H či:ʔ^L*
    passed few   days   were eggs of   them when^began children

    ko:ʔ^MR ga^MR ča^Mnéʔ^L kíʔ^H =i
    to^play toy   inside   place their

11. *hą^L lą́:^M   =i ʔi̯:^L k^yą́:^H či:ʔ^L   go^Lná:^M   ča^Mnéʔ^L kí^L*
    then thought they who of   children are^coming inside   place

    =n go^Lko:ʔ^L ga^MR
    my to^play toy

12. *ma^Llä^Lmé:ʔ^L^zë́^H =i to:ʔ^L ʔa:^MR či:ʔ^L   ča^Mnéʔ^L kíʔ^H*
    were^sad   they scatter spread children inside   place

    =i
    their

8. So they put them under a bowl.

9. They kept on going to their place (ranch).

10. A few days passed that the eggs were in their place, when kids began to play with toys in their house.

11. They thought, "Whose kids are coming to my house to play with toys?"

12. They were sad that the kids were leaving their things scattered in their house.

8. Así que, los pusieron debajo de un tazón.

9. Siguieron su camino hacia su lugar (rancho).

10. Hacía unos días que los huevos estaban en su lugar, cuando unos niños comenzaron a jugar con sus juguetes en su casa.

11. Ellos pensaron: —¿De quién son los niños que vienen a nuestra casa a jugar con juguetes?

12. Estaban tristes porque los niños estaban dejando sus cosas regadas en la casa.

13. *<pero>* *lä̌^{L}* *lá^H* *<sábado>* *<domingo>* *tä̠:ʔ^M*   *ba^M*
    but   like was Saturday   Sunday   were^there   (EMP)

    za^L   *ma^{L}g^{y}ʉ̠:ʔ^L*
    people old

14. *sá^L* *čạ̈:^{L}*   *či:ʔ^L*   *za^{L}ná̠:^{H}*
    not there^are children went

15. *hạ̈^{L}* *gá^{L}žá^M* *=i* *hu:^{H}* *lä̌^{L}ʉ́:^{M}*   *=i* *ča^{M}h^{w}e̠^{H}* *he:^{M}* *ia^{L}nä̠:^{LR}*
    then talked   they word the^two them   road   (LOC) came^back

    =i
    they

16. *čé^{M}máʔ^M* *gá^{L}žá^{L}ná̠:^{H}* *či:ʔ^L*   *ʔö̠:^{H}*   *ʔʉ́^{H}*
    if   arrived   children tomorrow day^after^tomorrow

    čạ̈:ʔ^M *=n* *máʔ^H*   *za^{M}hme:^{M}* *=n* *hu:^{H}* *kíʔ^H* *čo:^{H}*   *=i*
    grab we   and^then go^tell   we word to   mother their

17. *čé^{M}máʔ^M* *sá^L* *gá^{L}žá^{L}ná̠:^{H}*   *=i* *ʔö̠:^{H}*   *ʔʉ́^{H}*
    if   not have^arrived they tomorrow day^after^tomorrow

    <lunes> *hä̠ʔ^M*   *hni^M*
    Monday   will^say we

13. But on Saturdays and Sundays
    the old people were home;

14. the kids didn't go.

15. So the two of them chatted on
    their way as they came back:

16. "If the kids arrive tomorrow
    or the next day, let's grab
    them and go tell their mother.

17. If they haven't arrived tomor-
    row or the next day, Monday
    we will say:

13. Pero los sábados y domingos que
    los viejecitos estaban en la casa,

14. los niños no iban.

15. Así platicaban los dos en el
    camino de vuelta:

16. —Si los niños llegan mañana o
    al día siguiente, los vamos a
    agarrar e ir a decirle a su mamá.

17. Si para mañana o pasado
    mañana no han venido, el
    lunes diremos:

18. $ia^{M}n\acute{o}{:}^{H}$ hni^{M} $ko{:}^{L}$ $n\acute{u}{:}^{M}$
let's^go we   one night

19. $hme{:}^{H}$ $={\textit{?}}$ $l\acute{o}{:}^{H}$ $hn\ddot{a}^{LR}$ $=n$ ka^{H} $={\textit{?}}$ $\textit{?}\acute{e}^{H}$
will^do you load of   us   will^carry you tortillas

20. $m\acute{a}\textit{?}^{H}$ $h\ddot{a}\textit{?}^{M}$ $=n$ $ia^{M}n\acute{o}{:}^{H}$ hni^{M} $ko{:}^{L}$ $n\acute{u}{:}^{M}$
so^that say   we   we^will^come we   one night

21. la^{L} ba^{M} $hi{:}\textit{?}^{H}$ $ia^{M}n\acute{o}{:}^{H}$ hni^{M} $hi{:}\textit{?}^{H}$ $\check{c}a^{M}\textit{?}o{:}^{M}$ $hm\ddot{i}{:}^{L}$ la^{L}
here (EMP) until we^will^come us   until edge   river this

$m\acute{a}\textit{?}^{H}$ $za^{M}n\ddot{o}{:}^{M}$ $=n$ $ka^{L}l\acute{a}\textit{?}^{M}$
and   will^return we   again

22. $l\acute{a}^{L}$ ha^{L} $hme{:}^{M}$ $=n$ ha^{L}
like that will^do we (PAUSE)

23. $ua^{M}h\ddot{e}{:}^{M}$ da^{M} hni^{M} $\textit{?}a^{L}\,\hat{}\,l\acute{a}^{L}$ $l\acute{e}^{M}$
let's^see (DDM) us   how   happen

24. <pero> <como> $s\acute{a}^{L}$ $\check{c}a{:}^{L}$ $\check{c}i{:}\textit{?}^{L}$ $g\acute{a}^{L}\check{z}\acute{a}^{L}n\acute{a}{:}^{H}$
but   since   not there^were children arrived

18. 'Let's go for one night.

19. Prepare our load, take tortillas,

20. and we will say let's go for one night'.

21. We will come this far, as far as the river's edge here and go back again.

22. Let's do like that.

23. Let's see what happens."

24. But since the kids did not arrive,

18. —Vámonos por una noche.

19. Prepararemos nuestra carga, llevaremos tortillas,

20. y diremos que nos vamos por una noche.

21. Vamos a ir hasta la orilla del río, de este lado, y regresaremos otra vez.

22. Vamos a hacer eso.

23. Vamos a ver qué pasa.

24. Pero siendo que los niños no llegaron,

25. *hạ^L há̱ʔ^M za^Lñü:ʔ^L ʔé^M*
 then said man that

26. *go^{HR} sá^L ia:^Lná̱:^M   =i*
 likely not will^come they

27. *ma:^{LR}   =n kọ:^L nǘ:^M móʔ^M hnä^{LR} =n*
 let's^go us one night ranch of us

28. *ní^H hạ^L   há̱ʔ^M më^M =i*
 okay (PAUSE) said wife his

29. *hạ^L gá^Lʔ^ya:ʔ^L =i žú^H ča^Mnéʔ^L kíʔ^H =i*
 then swept she well inside place their

30. *ʔe^L <lunes> hạ^L*
 that Monday (PAUSE)

31. *hạ^L ga^M gá^Lhné^M =i ʔa:ʔ^M kíʔ^H =i*
 then more shut they door of them

32. *gá^Lʔ^wẹ:^L =i gá^Lná̱:^H =i*
 left they went they

25. the man said:

26. "I don't think they will come.

27. Let's go for one night to our
  ranch."

28. "Okay," his wife said.

29. So she swept their house well.

30. It was Monday.

31. Then they shut their door,

32. they exited, they left.

25. el hombre dijo:

26. —Creo que no van a venir.

27. Vamos al rancho por una
  noche.

28. —Bueno —dijo su esposa.

29. Así que, barrió la casa bien.

30. Era lunes.

31. Entonces cerraron su puerta,

32. y salieron, se fueron.

33. *ma^{L}lá^L*   *hë:^{MR}* *či:ʔ^L*   *ma^{L}ʔ^{w}ę́:^{L}* =*i*   *gá^{L}h^{y}ą́:^{H}*   *či:ʔ^L*
was^done   saw   children   left   they came^down   children

ʔ^{w}ą́^{H}
ground

34. *gá^{L}lǿ:^{H}* =*i*   *ko:ʔ^{MR}* =*i*   *ga^{MR}* =*i*
began   they to^play   they   toy   their

35. *ko^{L}ʔ^{w}ę́:^{M}*   *žú^H*   *ba^M*   *tą̈:ʔ^M*   =*i*   *ma^{M}iá^{L}nä:^{LR}*   *za^L*
little^while   good   (EMP)   were^there   they   when^returned   people

hü:^{M}
owner

36. *hą^L*   *hą́ʔ^M* *za^L*   *ʔé^M*   *ma^{L}hą́:^{L}* =*n*   *ʔną́ʔ^M*
then   said   person   that   captured   I   you

37. *ʔną́ʔ^M* *ba^M*   *na^L*   *hme:^{L}*   =*ʔ*   *ʔną́ʔ^M* *ta^M*   *na^L*
you   (EMP)   there   are^doing   you   you   work   that

38. *to:ʔ^L*   *ʔa:^{MR}*   =*ʔ*   *ča^{M}néʔ^L* *kí^L*   =*n*
scatter   spread   you   inside   place   my

33. When the kids saw them leave, they got down to the ground.

34. They began to play with their toys.

35. They were there for a good little bit when the owners came back.

36. Then the man said: "I have captured you.

37. You are the ones doing that work,

38. you are messing up my house."

33. Cuando los niños los vieron salir, se bajaron al piso.

34. Comenzaron a jugar con los juguetes.

35. Habían estado allá por un buen rato, cuando los dueños regresaron.

36. Entonces, el hombre dijo: —Les agarré.

37. Ustedes son los que están haciendo eso.

38. Ustedes están desarreglando mi casa.

39. *sá^L ča^L ʔe^L ko:ʔ^{MR} =n kʸá^H =ʔ ma^{LR}ʔʸa:^{M}*
    not is   what bothered I   place your grandmother

40. *ga^{MR} ba^M hnä̰^{M} ko:ʔ^{MR} =n*
    toys (EMP) our   areˆplaying we

41. *tá^L hme:ʔ^{LR} =ʔ hnä:ʔ^H*
    don't do   you us

42. *zo:^{M} hnä:ʔ^H he:^{M} hʸóʔ^M ba^M*
    willˆgo we   (LOC) other (EMP)

43. *gá^{L}ʔʷé̤:^{L} ba^M či:ʔ^L gá^{L}ná̰:^{H}*
    left   (EMP) children went

44. *ma^{M}gá^{L}ná̰:^{H} či:ʔ^L ha̰^{L} gá^{L}hé̤:^{H} za^L ma^{L}gʸṵ:ʔ^L kʷa:ʔ^L kíʔ^H*
    whenˆleft   children then looked person old   bowl his

45. *če^M sá^L má^{L}ka̰^{L} či:ʔ^L hlï:^{L} kíʔ^H =i*
    if   not took   children eggs of   him

39. "I haven't bothered anything
    of yours, Grandma,

40. we are playing with our toys.

41. Don't do anything to us,

42. we will go elsewhere."

43. The kids exited and left.

44. When the kids left, the old
    man looked at his bowl,

45. had the kids not taken his
    eggs?

39. —Yo no he tocado nada tuyo,
    abuelita.

40. Estamos jugando con nuestros
    juguetes.

41. No nos hagas nada.

42. Iremos a otro lado.

43. Los niños salieron, y se fueron.

44. Cuando se fueron los niños, el
    viejecito miró su tazón,

45. ¿no se habrían llevado los
    niños sus huevos?

46. *kʸa:ʔ^H ba^M hlï:^L tä:ʔ^M*
shells (EMP) eggs were

47. *li:^MR má^Lnë:ʔ^H ba^M lá^H*
apparent were^opened (EMP) was

48. *lá̧^L lá^H he:^M gá^Lʔʷȩ̈:^L ča:ʔ^M ba^M lá^H*
like is (LOC) left chicken (EMP) was

49. *gü̧:^L ʔé^M ba^M ma^Mtä̧:ʔ^M néʔ^L hlï:^L ha̧^L*
children those (EMP) were inside eggs those

50. *ha̧^L mó^Lsó^L gá^Lkó:ʔ^H =i ga^MR =i*
then no^longer played they toys their

51. *lá̧^L gá^Lʔná^M ha̧^L ba^M ma^Mgá^Lʔʷȩ̈:^L či:ʔ^L pi:ʔ^H ʔé^M*
like stopped (PAUSE) (EMP) when^left children little those

52. *gá^Lta̧:ʔ^LR =i hʷȩ̈^H gá^Lnä̧:^H =i ʔno:^L =i ta^M*
stood they road went they looking^for they work

46. Only the shells were there.

47. It was apparent they were
opened,

48. like it is where chicks exit it
was.

49. Those kids had been in the
eggs.

50. So they no longer played with
their toys.

51. It all stopped when the
children exited.

52. They set out on the road, they
went looking for work.

46. Nada más las cáscaras estaban
allá,

47. Era aparente que estaban
partidas,

48. como si fuera el lugar de
donde los pollitos habían salido.

49. Esos niños habían estado
dentro de los huevos.

50. Así que, ellos ya no jugaron
con sus juguetes.

51. Todo se terminó cuando los
niños salieron.

52. Se fueron por el camino;
andaban buscando un trabajo.

53. *he:^{M} ha̧^{L} gá^{L}hȩ:^{H} za^L či:ʔ^L ʔé^M ča^{M}h^{w}ë^H*
(LOC) there met   person children those road

54. *ha̧^{L} há̧ʔ^M za^L ʔé^M ʔa^L gá^{L}ná̧:^{M} =ʔ ʔná̧ʔ^M*
then said person that where are^going you you

55. *ʔnö:^{L} hnä:ʔ^H ta^M hme:^{M} hnä:ʔ^H*
are^looking^for we   work will^do we

56. *ʔe^{L}ha̧^{L} há̧ʔ^M za^L ʔé^M ma:^{LR} =n ta^M kí^L =n má̧ʔ^H*
thus   said person that let's^go us work of me and

      go^{M}hme:^{H} =ʔ ta^M kí^L =n
      will^go^do you work of me

57. *ha̧^{L} há̧ʔ^M či:ʔ^L pi:ʔ^H ʔé^M sá^L ʔlá̧:^{M} ta^M k^{y}á^H =ʔ*
then said children little those not much work of   you

      žá^L čá̧ʔ^M
      will^run^out immediately

53. There the children met a man on the road.	53. Allí, en la carretera, los niños se encontraron con un hombre.
54. The man said: "Where are you going?"	54. El hombre dijo: —¿A dónde van?
55. "We are obtaining work."	55. —Estamos buscando trabajo.
56. Then the man said: "Let's go do my work and you can go do my work."	56. Entonces el hombre dijo: —Vamos a trabajar, y ustedes pueden ir a hacer mi trabajo.
57. The little children said: "You don't have a lot of work, it will quickly run out."	57. Los niños chiquitos dijeron: —Usted no tiene suficiente trabajo; enseguida se va a acabar.

58. $ʔe^Lha^L$ $há̱ʔ^M$ za^L $ʔe^L$ $sá^L$ $ča^L$ $h^{wë̈H}$ $mó^L$ $ča^L$ $tá^L$
thus   said   person that not is   road no^longer is   toward

na^L
there

59. $če^Mmáʔ^M$ $gá^Lnǎ̱^{.H}$ $ʔnǎ̱ʔ^M$ $tá^L$ na^L
if   go   you   toward there

60. $he^{.M}$ na^L $g^{yá H}$ $mï^{.L}$ $tó̱^H$ $že^M$ $kú̱ːʔ^L$ $=i$ $ʔnǎ̱ʔ^M$
(LOC) there sits   eagle two heads will^eat   he you

61. $sá^L$ $ča̱ː^{.L}$ za^L $gá^Lnä̈^{.M}$ $tá^L$ na^L
not there^are people go   toward there

62. <pero> $nï^{.LR}$ $=n$ $na^Mhě̈^{.H}$ $=n$ $ko̱ː^L$ $há̱ʔ^M$ $čiːʔ^L$
but   will^go I   will^go^see I   once said kid

63. $ʔe^Lha^L$ $he^{.M}$ $gá^Lnǎ̱^{.H}$ $=i$ $gá^Lʔno̱ːʔ^L$ $=i$ $u̱ïː^L$
thus   (LOC) went   they looked^for   they vine

64. $gá^Lhmé^{.M}$ $=i$ $mïːʔ^L$
made   they baskets

---

58. Then the man said: "There is no longer a road that way.

59. If you continue that way,

60. there is a two-headed eagle there who will eat you.

61. People don't go that way."

62. "But I am going to see once," said the kid.

63. So as they went they looked for vines.

64. They made baskets.

58. Entonces el hombre dijo: —Ya no hay camino por ese lado.

59. Si siguen por ese lado,

60. hay un águila de dos cabezas allá, y les comerá.

61. La gente no va por ese camino.

62. —Pero yo voy a ver solamente una vez —dijo el niño.

63. Mientras iban, buscaban bejucos.

64. Ellos hicieron canastas.

65. *gá^{L}to:ʔ^L =i žĕ^M =i mášʔ^H sá^L ʔíʔ^H mï:^{L}
    put^in   they head their so^that not would^prick eagle

66. mï:ʔ^L na^{L}ʔä^M žĕ^M či:ʔ^L hạ^L sá^L gá^{L}ʔiʔ^{LR}
    baskets had^in head children thus not pricked

67. hạ^L ča^L mï:ʔ^L lá^{L}hị:ʔ^H na^L
    then is baskets until   now

68. gá^{L}ŋĕ̇:^{M} =i h^{w}ë̇^{H}
    went they road

69. ma^{M}gá^{L}ŋĕ̇:^{M} =i h^{w}ë̇^{H} hạ^L hậʔ^M či:ʔ^{L}mĕ^M ʔĕ^M hu^{H}ta
    when^went they road then said girl   that extremely

    lä^{L}kị:^{L} zĕ̇^{L} =n
    dry   heart I

70. <pero> sá^L ča^L hmï:^{L} ča^L
    but   not was water was

---

65. They put them on their heads so the eagle couldn't prick them.

66. The baskets had the kids' heads in them, thus they didn't get pricked.

67. And so there are baskets to this day.

68. They went along on the road.

69. As they went along the road the girl said, "Wow! I am really thirsty."

70. But there wasn't any water.

---

65. Se las pusieron en la cabeza para que el águila no les pudiera picar.

66. Las canastas tenían dentro las cabezas de los niños, y así no les picó.

67. Y por eso hay canastas hasta hoy.

68. Siguieron su camino en la carretera.

69. Cuando iban por el camino, la niña dijo: —¡Ay! Tengo mucha sed.

70. Pero no había nada de agua.

71. *gá^{L}ná:^{H}*   *g^{y}í?^{H}*   *ko:^{L}*   *nï:?^{MR}*   *ma^{M}gá^{L}tê:^{M}*   =*i*   *he:^{M}*   *?la^L*
went   still   one   distance   when^reached   they   place   was^lying

    ko:^{L}   *hmï:^{L}to:^{L}*
    one   water^hole

72. *ha^L*   *há?^{M}*   *či:?^{L}ñü:?^{L}*   *?é^M*   *na^{M}ŋï:^{LR}*   *da^M*   *hná^M*   *k^{y}a:?^{M}*   *kí?^{H}*
then   said   boy   that   will^go^ask   (DDM)   I   bowl   from

    za^L   *hü:^{M}*
    person   owner

73. *má?^{H}*   *?i:?^{M}*   =*n*   *hmï:^{L}*   *k^{y}a:?^{M}*   *k^{y}a:?^{M}*
so^that   will^drink   we   water   with   bowl

74. <*pero*>   *sá^L*   *gá^{L}lá^{L}bé^M*   *zê^H*   *či:?^{L}mê^M*
but   not   endured   heart   girl

75. *gá^L?í:?^{H}*   =*i*   *hmï:^{L}*   *k^{y}a:?^{M}*   *?o:^{M}*   =*i*
drank   she   water   with   mouth   her

76. *ma^{M}há?^{H}*   *či:?^{L}ñü:?^{L}*   *ha^L*   *gá^{L}hé^H*   =*i*   *kí?^{H}*   *či:?^{L}mê^M*
when^came^home   boy   then   bawled^out   he   to   girl

71. They went on a bit when they arrived where there was a water hole.

72. The boy said, "I will go ask for a bowl from the owner

73. so we can drink water with a bowl."

74. But the girl couldn't endure.

75. She drank water with her mouth (in the water).

76. When the boy came back, he scolded the girl.

71. Siguieron un poquito más. Cuando llegaron a donde había un hoyo con agua,

72. el niño dijo: —Iré a pedir un tazón al dueño

73. para que podamos tomar agua con un tazón.

74. Pero la niña no pudo aguantar.

75. Ella tomó agua con su boca (poniendo su boca en el agua).

76. Cuando el muchacho regresó, regañó a la niña.

77. $ʔe^Lla^H$ $ma^Lʔí:ʔ^M$ $= ʔ$
    why   drank   you

78. $ʔe^Lla^H$ $sá^L$ $ma^Lhọ:^M$ $= ʔ$
    why   not waited   you

79. $gá^Lką^H$ $= i$ $só ʔ^M$ $ʔí:^M$ $në^M$ $hmï:^L$
    carried he   slime   on   top   water

80. $gá^Lʔú:^H$ $= i$ $mo^Lnë^M$ $či:ʔ^Lmë́^M$
    put   he   face   girl

81. $lá́^Lgá^Lʔẹ:^H$ $hạ^L$ ba^M $mo^Lnë^M$ $= i$ $lá́^Lhị:ʔ^H$ $ná^H$
    still^ruined then (EMP)   face   her until   now

82. $kọ:^L$ $nï:ʔ^{MR}$ ga^M $gá^Lná:^H$ $= i$ $gá^Lzá:^H$ $h^wë̈^H$
    one distance more went   they ended   road

83. $he:^M$ $hạ^L$ $gá^Ltẹ:^M$ $= i$ $kọ:^L$ $ta^Lʔmï:^L$ $ča^Mʔlo:^L$
    (LOC) there reached they one base   boulder

77. "Why did you drink?

78. Why didn't you wait?"

79. He took some slime which was on the water,

80. he put it on the girl's face.

81. Her face was ruined from that time to this day.

82. They went on a bit more, the road ran out.

83. There they arrived at the base of a boulder.

77. —¿Por qué la tomaste?

78. ¿Por qué no esperaste?

79. Tomó algo del fango que había en el agua,

80. lo puso en la cara de la niña.

81. Su cara se arruinó por ese fango, hasta hoy.

82. Ellos siguieron un poco más, la carretera se terminó.

83. Allí llegaron a la base de una roca.

84. *he:ᴹ hạᴸ gáᴸzá:ᴴ hʷëᴴ*
(LOC) there ended road

85. *<pero> hmé:ᴸ gʸíʔᴴ ʔü:ᴹzëᴸ zaᴸná:ᴴ =i*
but were^doing still thought will^go they

86. *<pero> ʔaᴸ^láᴹ léᴹ sáᴸ sá:ᴸ =i*
but how will^be^possible not go^up they

87. *<pero> <como> gáᴸná:ᴴ pi:ʔᴸ <i> gáᴸná:ᴴ iaᴹsï:ʔᴸ*
but since went swallow and went bat

88. *ʔeᴸhạᴸ gáᴸʔlë:ʔᴹ =i kʸạ:ʔᴹ iaᴹsï:ʔᴸ*
thus talked he with bat

89. *gáᴸɲí:ᴹ =i hu:ᴴ čeᴹ sáᴸ kʸáʔᴴ =ʔ ʔnáʔᴹ háʔᴹ =i*
asked he word ? not are^hungry you you said he

90. *ʔeᴸhạᴸ háʔᴹ iaᴹsï:ʔᴸ kʸáʔᴴ hnä:ʔᴴ*
thus said bat are^hungry we

84. There the road ended.

85. But they were still thinking about continuing on.

86. But how was it possible, they couldn't go up.

87. But since a swallow went and a bat went,

88. so he talked with the bat.

89. He asked, "Are you not hungry?" he said.

90. Then the bat said, "We are hungry."

84. Allí terminó el camino.

85. Pero ellos todavía seguían pensando en seguir.

86. Pero ¿cómo sería posible, si no podían subir?

87. Pero, siendo que una golondrina y un murciélago fueron,

88. habló (el muchacho) con el murciélago.

89. Le preguntó: —¿No tienen hambre? —les dijo.

90. Entonces dijo el murciélago: —Tenemos hambre.

91. k^wa^{LR} $=n$ $h^w\ddot{e}^H$ $go^Lku{:}?^H$ $=?$ $m\ddot{i}^Hh\underset{.}{i}{:}?^L$
    will^give I   permission go^eat you berry

92. $\check{c}a^Lmi{:}?^L$ $go^Lk\acute{u}{:}?^H$ $=?$
    many   go^eat   you

93. $s\acute{a}^L$ $l\acute{e}^M$ $ku{:}?^{LR}$ $=n$ $\check{c}a^Lmi{:}?^L$
    not will^be^possible will^eat I   much

94. $s\acute{a}^L$ $\check{c}a^L$ $he{:}^M$ $tu{:}^{LR}$ $=n$ $h\acute{\underset{.}{a}}?^M$ $ia^Ms\ddot{\underset{.}{i}}{:}?^L$
    not is   place will^defecate I   said bat

95. $t\acute{\underset{.}{a}}^L$ $ua^Mg\underset{.}{a}?^H$ $=?$ $go^Lku{:}?^H$ $=?$ ba^M $?ne^L$
    don't afraid   you go^eat you (EMP) you

96. $n\acute{\underset{.}{a}}^H$ k^wa^{LR} $=n$ $he{:}^M$ $tu{:}^H$ $=?$ $n\acute{\underset{.}{a}}^H$
    now will^give I   place will^defecate you now

97. $n\acute{i}^H$ $h\underset{.}{a}^L$ $h\acute{\underset{.}{a}}?^M$ $ia^Ms\ddot{\underset{.}{i}}{:}?^L$
    okay (PAUSE) said bat

98. $?e^Lh\underset{.}{a}^L$ $g\acute{a}^Ln\acute{\underset{.}{a}}{:}^H$ $=i$
    thus   went   they

91. "I give you permission, go eat
    the berries.

92. Go eat a lot."

93. "I can't eat a lot.

94. There is no place for me to
    defecate," said the bat.

95. "Don't be afraid, you go eat.

96. I will give you a place to defe-
    cate now."

97. "Okay," said the bat.

98. Then they went.

91. —Les doy permiso. Vayan a
    comer los frutitos.

92. Vayan a comer bastante.

93. —Yo no puedo comer mucho.

94. No hay lugar para que yo vaya
    a defecar —dijo el murciélago.

95. —No tengas miedo. Vete a comer.

96. Te daré un lugar para defecar
    ahora.

97. —Bueno —dijo el murciélago.

98. Entonces, se fueron.

99. *ma^Mgá^Lžá^Lnä:^{LR}* =*i*   *ha^L*   *há?^M* =*i*
   when^arrived   they then said   they

100. *?a^L*   *tu:^{LR}*   =*n*
   where will^defecate I

101. *hu^Hta*   *uí:^M*   *tú?^L*   =*n*
   extremely hurts stomach my

102. *?e^Lha^L gá^Lk^wá^M* =*i he:^M*   *gá^Ltú:^M*   *ia^Msị:?^L ?ñí:^M ?ü:^M*
   thus   gave   he place defecated bat   itself base

   ?lo:^L   *ha^L*
   boulder that

103. <*pero*> *sá^L gá^Lhmá:^H ta^M*
   but   not served   work

104. *sá^L gá^Lk^wá:^H hё^{LR} ?ma^L hị:?^L*
   not grow   tall tree berry

105. *gá^L?é:^L ta^M*   *kí?^H* =*i*
   ruined work of   his

99. When they arrived back they said:

100. "Where will I defecate?

101. My stomach really hurts."

102. Then he gave a place for the bat to defecate right at the base of the boulder.

103. But it didn't serve.

104. The berry tree didn't grow tall.

105. His work was ruined.

99. Cuando llegaron de nuevo, dijo:

100. —¿Dónde voy a defecar?

101. Mi estómago me duele de veras.

102. Entonces (el muchacho) le dio un lugar al murciélago para que defecara: mero en la base de la roca.

103. Pero no sirvió.

104. El árbol de bayas no creció mucho.

105. Su trabajo se arruinó.

106. ha^L $gá^L\eta í{:}^H$ $=i$ $hu{:}^H$ $ka^Llá\emph{?}^M$ $\check{c}e^M$ $sá^L$ $l\acute{e}?^H$ $=?$ $ku{:}?^H$
    then asked he word again do not know^how you will^eat

    $=?$ $m\ddot{i}{:}^H$ $?ma^Lhe^L$
    you fruit berry^tree

107. $l\acute{i}{:}?^L$ ba^M $hn\mathring{a}^M$ $ku{:}?^{LR}$ $=n$ $mi{:}?^L$
    know^how (EMP) I   eat I little

108. $?e^Lha^L$ $h\acute{a}?^M$ $=i$ $go^Lku{:}?^H$ $\check{c}a^Lmi{:}?^L$ $má?^H$ k^wa^{LR} $=n$ $he{:}^M$
    thus   said he go^eat   many   and will^give I   where

    $tu{:}^H$ $=?$ $ka^Llá?^M$
    will^defecate you again

109. $h\acute{a}?^M$ $=i$ $s\acute{i}{:}?^L$ $=i$ $ia^Ms\underset{.}{i}{:}?^L$
    said he told he bat

110. ni^H ha^L $h\acute{a}?^M$ $=i$
    okay (PAUSE) said he

111. $gá^Ln\mathring{a}{:}^H$ $=i$
    went he

106. So he asked again, "Do you know how to eat berries?"	106. Así que, preguntó otra vez: —¿Sabes cómo comer bayas?
107. "I know how to eat them somewhat."	107. —De alguna manera, yo sé cómo comerlas.
108. So he said, "Go eat a lot and I will give you a place to defecate again,"	108. Así que (el muchacho) dijo: —Ve y come otra vez, y yo te daré un lugar para defecar otra vez
109. he told the bat.	109. —dijo al murciélago.
110. "Okay," he said.	110. —Bueno —dijo él.
111. He went.	111. Se fue.

112. *ma^Miá^Lnä:^LR*   = *i*   *ha̧^L*   *há̧ʔ^M*   = *i*
when^returned they then said   they

113. *uí:^M*   *túʔ^L*   = *n*   *ka^Llá̧ʔ^M*
hurts stomach my   again

114. *ʔe^Lha̧^L*   *há̧ʔ^M*   *či:ʔ^L*   *ʔé^M*   *he:^M*   *la^L*   *tú:^M*   *ka^Llá̧ʔ^M*
thus   said   kid   that (LOC) here defecate again

115. *ha̧^L*   *gá^Ltú:^M*   *ia^Msi̧:ʔ^L*   *ʔü:^M*   *ʔlo:^L*   *ha̧^L*
then   defecated bat   base boulder that

116. *he:^M*   *ha̧^L*   *gá^Lʔia^L*   *ʔma^Lhe^L*
(LOC) there sprang^up berry^tree

117. *gá^Lbéʔ^H*   *gá^Lg^yó̧ʔ^H*   *zóʔ^M*   *ʔlo:^L*   *ha̧^L*
doubled wrapped against boulder that

118. *ŋó:^H*   *gá^Ltȩ̈^M*   *në^M*   *ʔlo:^L*
went to^reach top boulder

112. When they came back they said:

113. "My stomach hurts again."

114. So the boy said, "Defecate here again."

115. So the bat defecated at the base of the boulder.

116. There a tree sprouted.

117. It wrapped around the boulder.

118. It almost reached the top of the boulder.

112. Cuando ellos vinieron de vuelta dijeron:

113. —Me duele el estómago otra vez.

114. Así que, dijo el niño: —Defeca aquí otra vez.

115. Así que, el murciélago defecó en la base de la roca.

116. Allá brotó un árbol.

117. Se enroscó alrededor de la roca.

118. Llegó casi a lo más alto de la roca.

119. $ʔe^L$ $ha̧^L$ $gá^Lʔa̧:^H$ $=i$
     *   that   pulled   they

120. $gá^Luí:^H$ $=i$ $zóʔ^M$ $ʔlo:^L$ $ha̧^L$ $lá^Lhi̧:ʔ^H$ $gá^Lʔʸa̧:^M$ $=i$ $gá^Ltȩ^M$
      climbed   they   against   boulder   that   until   popped   they   arrived

    $në^M$ $gü:ʔ^H$
    upon   up

121. $he:^M$ $ha̧^L$ $gʸá^H$ $ha̧:^L$ za^L $ʔe^Lha̧^L$ $há̧ʔ^M$ $či:ʔ^L$ $če^M$ $ča^L$
      (LOC)   there   sat   one   person   thus   said   kid   ?   there^is

    ta^M $hme:^{LR}$ $=n$ $kʸá^H$ $=ʔ$
    work   will^do I   for   you

122. $ča^L$ ba^M ta^M $há̧ʔ^M$ za^L
      there^is   (EMP)   work   said   person

123. $sá^L$ $go^Lnä:^H$ $=ʔ$ $ʔná̧ʔ^M$ $ko̧^Lho̧ʔ^M$ ba^M
      not   will^go   you   you   together   (EMP)

124. $če^M$ $hme:^H$ $=ʔ$
      ?   will^do   you

119. They pulled on it,

119. Ellos lo jalaron,

120. they climbed up the boulder until they popped up at the top of the the boulder.

120. y subieron a la roca hasta que aparecieron encima de la roca.

121. There sat a man. The boy said, "Is there work we can do for you?"

121. Allí estaba sentado un hombre. El niño dijo: —¿Hay algún trabajo que podemos hacer para usted?

122. "There is work," said the man.

122. —Sí hay trabajo —dijo el hombre—.

123. "But you will not go together."

123. Pero no van a ir juntos.

124. Will you do it?"

124. ¿Lo harán?

125. $hme:^{LR} =n$ $\mathit{?e}^L$ na^L $\mathit{?nó:}^H =n$ $h\mathring{a}\mathit{?}^M$ $\check{c}i:\mathit{?}^L$ $\mathit{?ê}^M$
will^do I   that there want I   said kid that

126. $\mathit{?e}^L$ la^L $go:^H$ $=\mathit{?}$ $\mathit{?ne}^L$ $h\mathring{a}\mathit{?}^M =i$ $s\mathring{i}:\mathit{?}^L =i$ $\check{c}i:\mathit{?}^L\tilde{n}\ddot{u}:^L$
* here will^go you you said he told he boy

127. $\mathit{?ne}^L$ $l\mathring{e}:^M$ $=\mathit{?}$ $\mathit{?}^y o:^L$
you will^become you sun

128. $<i>$ $\mathit{?e}^L$ la^L $go:^H =\mathit{?}$ $\mathit{?ne}^L$ $h\mathring{a}\mathit{?}^M =i$ $s\mathring{i}:\mathit{?}^L =i$ $\check{c}i:\mathit{?}^L m\mathring{e}^M$
and * here go you you said he told he girl

129. $\mathit{?ne}^L$ $l\mathring{e}:^M$ $=\mathit{?}$ $s\ddot{i}:\mathit{?}^L$
you will^become you moon

130. $\mathit{?e}^L$ $ma^L la^L$ $mo^L n\ddot{e}^M =\mathit{?}$ $h\mathring{a}\mathit{?}^M$ za^L $\mathit{?é}^M$ $s\mathring{i}:\mathit{?}^L =i$
what was^done face   your said person that told he

$\check{c}i:\mathit{?}^L m\mathring{e}^M$
girl

131. $g\mathring{a}^L \mathit{?ú}:^H =i$ $hm\ddot{i}:^L$ $só\mathit{?}^M$ $\check{c}a^M h^w \ddot{e}^H$ $he:^M$ $i\mathring{a}^L n\mathring{o}:^H$ $hn\ddot{a}:\mathit{?}^H$
put   he water dirty road   where were^coming we

125. "I will do it. That is what I want," said the boy.

126. "Here you will go," he said, he told the boy.

127. "You will be the sun.

128. And here you will go," he said, he told the girl.

129. "You will be the moon.

130. What happened to your face?" the man said, he asked the girl.

131. "He put dirty water (on it) on the road where we were coming."

125. —Yo lo haré. Eso es lo que quiero —dijo el niño.

126. —Aquí vas a ir —dijo, le dijo al niño.

127. —Tú serás el sol.

128. Y aquí vas tú —él dijo, le dijo a la niña—.

129. Tú serás la luna.

130. ¿Qué te pasó en la cara? —el hombre dijo; le preguntó a la niña.

131. —Él me puso agua sucia (encima) en el camino donde veníamos.

132. *Ɂña:^L zë́^H*   =*i* *hạ^L*   *Ɂe^Lhạ^L* *sá^L* *go:^H*   =*Ɂ* *k^ya:Ɂ^M* =*i*
     mean heart he   (PAUSE) thus   not will^go you with   him

     kọ^Lhǫ́Ɂ^M
     together

133. *Ɂe^L* *la^L* *ba^M*   *go:^H* =*Ɂ* *Ɂne^L*
     *   here (EMP) go   you you

134. *Ɂe^L* *la^L* *zó:^H*   =*i*
     *   here will^go he

135. *hnã́^M* *hme:^LR*   =*n* *ɁíɁ^L*
     I   will^make I   decisions

136. <*porque*> *má^L* =*n* *k^we:^L* *Ɂña:^L* *zë^L*   =*i*
     because   know I   well mean heart he

137. *hạ^L* *gá^Lhmé:Ɂ^L* =*i* *Ɂne^L* *ča^Mh^wë^H* *he:^M*   *iá^Lnã́:^H* =*Ɂ* *Ɂnã́Ɂ^M*
     thus mistreated he you road   where came   you you

138. *hạ^L* *sá^L* *go:^H*   =*Ɂ* *k^ya:Ɂ^M* =*i* *kọ^Lhǫ́Ɂ^M*
     thus not will^go you with   him together

132. "He is mean, thus you will not
     go together with him.

133. Here is where you will go.

134. Here is where he will go.

135. I am the one who makes
     decisions.

136. Because I know well that he is
     mean,

137. thus he mistreated you on the
     road where you came.

138. Thus you won't go together
     with him.

132. —Él es malo; por eso tú no
     vas a ir con él.

133. Aquí es donde vas a ir.

134. Y aquí es donde él va a ir.

135. Yo soy el que hace las
     decisiones.

136. Porque yo sé bien que él es
     malo,

137. por eso te maltrató en el
     camino en que venías.

138. Por eso tú no irás con él.

139. *tá^L   ná^H he:^M hạ:^L sï:ʔ^L ga^M hḗ:^L   =ʔ ʔníʔ^M*
     toward   now   (LOC) a   month   more will^meet you you^him

     kọ:^L hmï:^L
     one   day

140. *lá̰^Lžú^H sá^L gá^Llá̰^Lhǫ̰́:ʔ^L zḛ́^H   =i k^yạ:ʔ^M ʔne^L hǎ́ʔ^M zá^H   ʔị:^L*
     since   not   patient   heart he with   you   said   person who

     gá^Lk^wá̰^M ta^M kíʔ^H =i ʔé^M
     gave   work of   him that

141. *kíʔ^H   ʔe^L gá^Lhmé:ʔ^L či:ʔ^L ʔé^M za^Lmḛ́^M ö̰:ʔ^HR =i ča^Mh^wё̈^H*
     because what mistreated kid   that woman   sister his road

     he:^M   iá^Lnǎ́:^H
     where came

142. *gá^Lʔú:^H =i hmï:^L sóʔ^M mo^Lnё̈^M =i*
     put   he water slime face   her

143. *ʔe^Lhạ^L sá^L gá^Lk^wá̰^M za^L   h^wё̈^H   ma^Mza^Lnǎ́:^H =i*
     thus   not   gave   person permission go   they

     kọ^Lhǫ̰́ʔ^M
     together

139. On up ahead, in a month, then
     you will meet him one day,

140. since he was not patient with
     you," said the man who gave
     them work.

141. Because the kid mistreated his
     sister on the way where they
     came,

142. he put slime on her face,

143. thus, the man didn't allow
     them to go together.

139. Más adelante, en un mes,
     entonces le encontrarás un día,

140. siendo que él no fue paciente
     contigo —dijo el hombre que
     les dio trabajo.

141. Porque el niño había
     maltratado a su hermana
     cuando estaban viniendo;

142. le había puesto fango en la
     cara;

143. por eso, el hombre no les
     permitió ir juntos.

144. *ʔe^Lhą^L na^Lʔę:^HR mo^Lnë^M =i lá̧^Lhi̧:ʔ^H ná^H*
     thus   is^ruined face   her until   now

145. *hë:^LR da^M   ʔná̧ʔ^M ua^Mrá̧ʔ^M há̧^H   =i ʔña:ʔ^M =i čé^Mmá̧ʔ^M sá^L*
     see   (DDM) you   when   comes it full it if   not

     zó:^M   ʔó^M   =ʔ
     straight heart you

146. *lá̧^L hą^L lá^H hu:^H kíʔ^H sï:ʔ^L kʸą:ʔ^M ʔʸo:^L*
     like that is   story about moon and   sun

144. Thus her face is ruined even   144. Por eso su cara está arruinada
     today.   hasta hoy.

145. Notice, all of you, when the   145. Fíjense todos ustedes, cuando
     moon is full again, if you don't   la luna esté llena otra vez, si
     believe it.   no lo creen.

146. That's the story about the   146. Esa es la historia de la Luna y
     moon and sun.   el Sol.

A Hired Hand Exchanges the King's Bull for a Wife

1. *ko̧:ᴸ ʔä̧ᴹ ha̧:ᴸ <mozo> maᴹhmé:ᴸ =i taᴹ kʸa̧:ʔᴹ*
   once time a hired^man used^to^do he work with

   ha̧:ᴸ <rei>
   a king

2. *<pero> <mozo> ʔéᴹ iá̧ᴸʔę́:ᴴ žúᴴ <hʷërte> čaᴹnëᴹ*
   but hired^man that came^out well strong before

   <rei>
   king

1. Once a hired man worked with a king.

2. Now the hired man came out well before the king.

1. Había una vez un hombre que trabajaba con un rey.

2. Este empleado lo hacía bien delante del rey.

45

3. *ma^Llä^L ʔï:^LR*   *ʔä̤:^M*   <*mozo*> *ʔé^M hmé:^L ta^M kíʔ^H*
   now^long^time   was^there hired^man that doing work of

   <*rei*> *ʔé^M*
   king   that

4. *hạ^L gá^Lto:ʔ^L* <*rei*> *go:^L* <*mozo*> *ʔé^M hé̤:^H*   =*i*
   then put^in   king   hands hired^man that was^watching he

   néʔ^L hnë̤^H
   inside pasture

5. *ma^Llá^H   k^wạta^MR kíʔ^H* =*i ʔe^L za^Lhï:ʔ^HR néʔ^L   hnë̤^H*
   now^was duty   of   him that to^weed inside pasture

6. *ma^Llá^H   k^wạta^MR kíʔ^H* =*i lé^M*   *më̤^MR   kíʔ^H k^ya^M*
   now^was duty   of   him will^be^possible medicine to   cattle

7. *ma^Llä^L ʔï:^LR ʔä̤:^M*   <*mozo*> *ʔé^M ma^Mgá^Lžó:^H* <*rei*>
   long^time   was^there hired^man that when^arrived king

   ʔé^M na^Mhë̤:^L k^ya^M zó^H k^yá̤:^H =*i*
   that saw   cattle male of   him

3. The hired man had been with the king a long time.	3. El empleado había estado con el rey por mucho tiempo.
4. So the king gave to the hired man the responsibility of watching the pasture.	4. Así que, el rey dio a su empleado la responsabilidad de cuidar el pastizal.
5. It was his duty to go weed the pasture.	5. Era su responsabilidad quitar la mala hierba del pastizal.
6. It was his duty to treat the cattle medically.	6. Era su responsabilidad dar medicina al ganado.
7. The hired man had been (on duty) for sometime when the king arrived to see his bull.	7. El empleado había estado (de responsable) por algún tiempo, cuando el rey llegó a ver su toro.

8. *hu^Hta gá^Ltî?^H^zê^H* <rei> *ma^Mgá^Lhȩ̂:^H* =*i k^ya^M zó^H k^yá̧:^H*
wow! liked   king   when^saw   he cattle male of

=*i*
him

9. *hu^Hta hlą:?^H ma^Llȩ̈:^MR k^ya^M*
wow! good   became   cattle

10. *kǫ:^L na^Mhë:^L   =i lá̧^L hą^L ba^M há?^M ?é^M*
just came^to^see   he like that (EMP) animals those

11. *há̧?^H   bî?^H ma^Mgá^Lhȩ̂:^H =i na^Mtȩ:^LR ba^M k^ya^M k^yá̧:^H*
came^back he   when^saw   he complete (EMP) cattle of

=*i*
him

12. *gá^Llá̧^L?ï̧:^LR ga^M ka^Llá̧?^M ma^Mgá^Lžó:^H hą:^L za^L lą:^MR k^ya^M*
later   more again   when^arrived a   person to^buy cattle

13. *hą^L gá^Lhá̧?^M* <mozo> *?é^M sá^L čą:^L k^ya^M čą:^L*
then said   hired^man that not are cattle are

8. Wow! He liked it when he
saw his bull.

9. Wow! The cattle had really become pretty.

10. He just came to see the
animals.

11. He came home when he saw
his cattle were complete.

12. Some more time passed when
a man arrived to buy cattle.

13. Then that hired man said,
"There aren't any."

8. De veras le gustó su toro
cuando lo vio.

9. El ganado se había puesto
muy bien.

10. Él había venido sólo a ver a
los animales.

11. Regresó a su casa cuando vio
que su ganado estaba completo.

12. Cuando pasó un poco de
tiempo, un hombre vino a
comprar ganado.

13. Entonces, el empleado dijo:
—No hay ganado.

14. <*pero*> *ma^Mgá^Lhȩ́:^H za^L* *ʔé^M ha̧:^L kʸa^M zó^H ʔä̧:^M he:^M*
but when^saw person that one cattle male was (LOC)

ha̧^L ha̧^L gá^Llá̧:^H =i
there then bought he

15. <*pero*> *sá^L ʔí:^H*   <*mozo*> *ʔé^M ma^Mʔnȩ́:^H =i*
but not did^agree hired^man that to^sell he

16. *ha̧^L há̧ʔ^M za^L* *ʔé^M ua^Mhme:^M =n si̧:^H ha̧^L čé^Mmá̧ʔ^M*
then said person that let's^make us swap (PAUSE) if

sá^L ʔnë:^H =ʔ
not sell you

17. *k^wa̧:^HR =n ha̧:^L za^Lmȩ́^M kʸá̧:^H =ʔ*
will^give I a woman to you

18. *ha̧^L há̧ʔ^M* <*mozo*> *ʔé^M lé^M*   *ba^M* <*pero*>
then said hired^man that will^be^possible (EMP) but

ha̧^L ia^Lhá̧:^L   =ʔ da^M ʔne^L za^Lmȩ́^M ʔé^M
(PAUSE) come^bring you (DDM) you woman that

14. Now when the man saw the bull there, he (wanted to) buy it.

gá^Llá̧:^H 'buy' indicates a strong desire to buy the bull rather than an actual purchase even though the gloss 'bought' indicates a purchase.

15. But the hired man didn't agree to sell him.

16. So the man said, "Let's swap if you won't sell him.

17. I will give a woman to you."

18. The hired man said, "That is fine but you bring the woman.

14. Pero, cuando el hombre vio al toro allí, lo (quiso) comprar.

gá^Llá̧:^H 'comprar' indica un deseo fuerte de comprar el toro más que el hecho de comprarlo, aún cuando la glosa 'comprar' indica obtención de algo.

15. Pero el empleado no estaba de acuerdo en venderlo.

16. Así que, el hombre dijo: —Vamos a cambiar, si no quieres venderlo.

17. Yo te daré una mujer.

18. El empleado dijo: —Está bien; pero trae la mujer.

19. $h\ddot{e}\ddot{\cdot}^{HR}$ $=n$ $\check{c}e^M$ $t\acute{i}?^{H\wedge}z\acute{e}^L$ $=n$
    will^see I if like I

20. ha^L $h\acute{a}?^M$ za^L $?\acute{e}^M$ $<lunes>$ $h^y\acute{o}?^M$ $<semana>$ $h\acute{a}^L$
    then said person that Monday next week will^come

    $=n$ ha^L
    I (PAUSE)

21. $n\acute{e}^H$ $h\ddot{a}\cdot^M$ $=n$ $?ne^L$ $h\acute{a}?^M$ $<mozo>$ $?\acute{e}^M$
    okay will^wait I you said hired^man that

22. $g\acute{a}^Lt\acute{e}^M$ $<lunes>$ ha^L $g\acute{a}^L\check{z}\acute{o}\cdot^H$ za^L $?\acute{e}^M$ $k^y a\cdot?^M$ $=i$
    arrived Monday (PAUSE) arrived person that with he

    $h\acute{o}\cdot^M m\ddot{\imath}\cdot^{HR}$ $=i$
    daughter his

23. hu^Hta $g\acute{a}^Lt\acute{i}?^{H\wedge}z\acute{e}^H$ $<mozo>$ $?\acute{e}^M$ $za^Lm\acute{e}^M$ $?\acute{e}^M$
    wow! liked hired^man that woman that

24. $g\acute{a}^L?e\cdot?^L$ $=i$ $g\acute{a}^Lk^w\acute{a}\cdot^H$ $=i$ $k^y a^M$ $z\acute{o}^H$ $k^y\acute{a}\cdot^H$ $<rei>$
    accepted he gave he cattle male of king

19. I will see if I like her."

19. Veré si me gusta.

20. The man said, "Monday of next week I will come."

20. El hombre dijo: —El lunes, o la próxima semana volveré.

21. "Okay, I will wait for you," said the hired man.

21. —Bueno, te esperaré —dijo el empleado.

22. Monday came and the man arrived with his daughter.

22. Llegó el lunes, y el hombre llegó con su hija.

23. My! How the hired man liked the woman!

23. ¡Ay! ¡Cómo le gustó la mujer al empleado!

24. He accepted and he gave him the king's bull.

24. Aceptó, y le dio el toro del rey.

25. *gá^{L}hą̂^{M} za^{L}mę́^{M} ʔé^M k^{y}ą:ʔ^M <mozo> ʔé^M*
stayed   woman   that   with   hired^man   that

26. *ma^{L}ŋę̈:^{M} hą^L sá^L ñe^L <mozo> ʔé^M ʔa^L^lą̂^{L} sî:ʔ^L*
after^that (PAUSE) not   know   hired^man   that   how   will^tell

     =*i* <rei> *ua^{M}ráʔ^M há^H =i hę̂:^{H} =i k^{y}a^M zó^H k^{y}ą̂:^{H} =i*
     he   king   when   came   he   see   he   cattle   male   of   him

27. *mi:ʔ^L hmï:^{M} ga^M gá^{L}lą̂^{L}ʔï:^{LR} ma^{M}gá^{L}žó:^{H} <rei> hë:^{LR}*
few   days   more   passed   when^arrived   king   look

     ka^{L}lą̂ʔ^M néʔ^L hnë^H kíʔ^H
     again   inside   pasture   his

28. *gá^{L}hę̂:^{H} =i k^{w}e:^{L} lą̂^{L}hę̂:^{L} k^{y}a^M k^{y}ą̂:^{H} =i*
saw   he   carefully   all   cattle   of   him

29. *sá^L čą:^{L} k^{y}a^M zó^H čą:^{L}*
not   was   cattle   male   was

---

25. The woman remained with the hired man.

26. After that the hired man didn't know what he would tell the king when he came to see his bull.

27. A few more days passed when the king arrived again to look at his pasture.

28. He carefully looked at his cattle.

29. The bull wasn't there.

25. La mujer se quedó con el empleado.

26. Después de eso, el empleado no sabía qué le iba a decir al rey cuando viniera a ver su toro.

27. Pasaron unos pocos días más cuando el rey vino otra vez a ver su pastizal.

28. Con mucho cuidado revisó su ganado.

29. El toro no estaba allá.

30. *hạ^L gá^Lhá̱ʔ^M \<rei\> sí:ʔ^L \<mozo\> ʔé^M na:^{HR} ba^M kʸa^M*
    then said   king   told   hired^man that where (EMP) cattle

zó^H
male

31. *hạ^L há̱ʔ^M \<mozo\> ʔị:^L ʔạ̈:^M   na^L   ʔa^L   ʔạ̈:^M*
    then said hired^man   he   is^there (PAUSE) where is^there

néʔ^L   nu:^L
inside woods

32. *ʔe^L   sá^L ma^Lhạʔ^{MR}   bíʔ^H há̱ʔ^M \<mozo\>*
    it^is^that not   has^come^back   he   said   hired^man

33. *sá^L tụ:^L^zé̱^H =i há̱ʔ^L   =i gá^Lmí^Lsé̱:^H =i*
    not   dared   he will^say   he exchanged   he

34. *hë:^{LR} da^M   če^M   há̱ʔ^M   =i há̱ʔ^M \<rei\>*
    see   (DDM) if   comes^back   he said   king

35. *ŋá:ʔ^H   bíʔ^H*
    went^home   he

30. The king said to the hired man, "Where is the bull?"

31. The hired man said, "He is there somewhere in the woods.

32. He just hasn't come back," said the hired man.

33. He didn't dare say he had exchanged him.

34. "You (watch and) see if he comes back," said the king.

35. He went home.

30. El rey le dijo a su empleado: —¿Dónde está el toro?

31. El empleado dijo: —Allá está, en algún lado en el bosque.

32. No ha vuelto —dijo el empleado.

33. No se atrevió a decir que lo había cambiado.

34. —Ve (y observa) si vuelve —dijo el rey.

35. Y se fue a su casa.

36. *ʔnë͏̈ᴸ hmï:ᴹ baᴹ ñe:ʔᴹ   =i maᴹgáᴸžó:ᴴ   =i kaᴸláʔᴹ*
    three days (EMP) wasˆgone he whenˆarrived he again

    žeᴸᴿˆzë́ᴴ   =i kʸaᴹ kʸ·ą̈:ᴴ =i
    thinkingˆabout he cattle of   him

37. *hąᴸ há͏̈ʔᴹ <rei> sí:ʔᴸ =i <mozo> maᴹgáᴸžó:ᴴ   =i*
    then said king   told he hiredˆman whenˆarrived he

    kaᴸláʔᴹ néʔᴸ hnë̈ᴴ   čeᴹ maᴸhąʔᴹᴿ kʸaᴹ zóᴴ
    again   inside pasture ?   came   cattle male

38. *sáᴸ čą:ᴸ há͏̈ʔᴹ <mozo> ʔéᴹ*
    not is   said hiredˆman that

39. *<pero> góʔᴸ   =i hmé:ʔᴴ =i hu:ᴴ kíʔᴴ <rei>*
    but   wasˆafraid he toˆtell he word to   king

40. *hąᴸ há͏̈ʔᴹ <rei> ži:ʔóᴹ =ʔ hąᴸ   máʔᴴ zaᴹʔnä:ʔᴹ =n*
    then said king   hurry you (PAUSE) and goˆlook   we

    kaᴸhü:ʔᴸ kʸaᴹ
    shortly   cattle

---

36. He was gone for three days, when he arrived again, thinking about his cattle.

37. So the king said to the hired man when he arrived again at the pasture, "Did the bull come back?"

38. "He is not here," said the hired man.

39. He was really afraid to tell the king (the truth).

40. Then the king said, "Hurry up let's go look for the bull right now.

36. Se fue por tres días. Cuando regresó, estaba pensando en su ganado.

37. Así, el rey dijo al empleado cuando volvió al pastizal: —¿Volvió el toro?

38. —No está aquí —dijo el empleado.

39. Él tenía mucho miedo de decir (la verdad) al rey.

40. Entonces le dijo el rey: —¡Apúrate! Vamos a buscar al toro ahorita mismo!

41. $\eta\acute{o}^{.H}$ $g\acute{a}^L l\acute{a}^L ?\ddot{\imath}^{.LR}$ la^L $h\mathring{a}?^M$ $<rei>$
    is^gone later   now said king

42. $n\acute{e}^H$ $h\mathring{a}?^M$ $<mozo>$
    okay said hired^man

43. $za^L ?maá^{.H\wedge}za^L n\acute{e}^H$ $=i$ $l\acute{a}^L$ ha^L $\check{z}\mathring{e}^{.LR}$ $=i$ $ka{:}?^{LR}$ $k\acute{\imath}?^H$
    was^dragging   he like that was^following he behind of

    $<rei>$
    king

44. $m\acute{o}^L s\acute{o}^L$ $?\ddot{\imath}^{.MR}$ $=i$ $z\acute{o}^{.H}$ $=i$ $za^L ?n\mathring{a}^{.?L}$ $=i$
    no^longer agreed he to^go he go^look he

45. $h\acute{e}^{.M}$ $=?$ $\tilde{n}e^L$ $=i$ $k^w e^{.L}$ $s\acute{a}^L$ $\check{c}a^{.L}$ $k^y a^M$ $\check{c}a^{.L}$
    because you knew he well not was cattle was

46. ha^L $d\acute{o}^L$ $g\acute{a}^L \eta\ddot{\imath}^{.M}$ $<rei>$ $?\acute{e}^M$ $hu{:}^H$ $k^w e^{.L}$ $k\acute{\imath}?^H$ $<mozo>$
    then * asked king that word carefully to hired^man

    $k^y \mathring{a}^{.H}$
    his

41. It has been a long time now,"
    said the king.

42. "Okay," said the hired man.

43. He was dragging along like so
    following behind the king.

44. He no longer wanted to go
    look for it,

45. because he knew well there
    was no bull.

46. Then the king asked his hired
    man carefully.

41. Ya ha pasado bastante tiempo
    —dijo el rey.

42. —Bueno —dijo el empleado.

43. Él iba como arrastrándose
    detrás del rey.

44. Él ya no quería ir a buscarlo,

45. porque él sabía muy bien que
    ya no había toro.

46. Entonces el rey interrogó
    cuidadosamente a su empleado.

47. *gá^{L}hǎʔ^M* =i ʔne^L <mozo> ma^{L}g^{y}ṳ:ʔ^L k^{y}á̱:^{L} =n sá^L ča^L
    said   he   you   hired^man   old   of   me   not   will^be

    ʔe^L hme:^{LR} =n k^{y}á^H =ʔ
    what   will^do   I   to   you

48. *hä̱ʔ^M* =ʔ čér^M má̱ʔ^M ma^{L}ʔnë̱:^{LR} =ʔ k^{y}a^M zó^H k^{y}á̱:^{L} =n
    say   you   if   *   sold   you   cattle   male   of   me

49. *ha̱^{L} ga^M gá^{L}tṳ:^{L}^zë̱^{H}* <mozo> ʔê^M gá^{L}hǎʔ^M ko̱:^{L} k^{y}e^M k^{y}a^M
    then   more   dared   hired^man   that   said   one   leg   cattle

    ko̱:^{L} k^{y}e^M ʔ^{y}a:^{LR}
    one   leg   woman

50. *gá^{L}ŋí̱:^{H}* ba^M <rei>   ma^{M}gá^{L}nú:^{M} lá̱^{L} ha̱^{L}
    laughed   (EMP)   king   when^heard   like   that

51. *čá̱ʔ^M*   ba^M gá^{L}lá̱^{L}zé̱:^{MR} <rei> hu:^{H} ha̱^{L}
    immediately   (EMP)   understood   king   word   (PAUSE)

52. *ha̱^{L} gá^{L}hǎ̱ʔ^M* =i na:^{HR} bíʔ^H ha̱^{L}
    then   said   he   where   she   (PAUSE)

---

47. He said, "You, my old hired man, I will not do anything to you.

48. Say it if you have sold my bull."

49. Finally, the hired man dared to say, "One cow's leg (for) one woman's leg."

50. The king laughed when he heard that.

51. Right away the king understood the word.

52. So he said, "Where is she?"

47. Él dijo: —A tí, mi empleado antiguo, no te voy a hacer nada.

48. Dime si tú vendiste mi toro.

49. Finalmente, el empleado se atrevió a decir: —Una pierna de vaca (por) una pierna de mujer.

50. El rey se rió cuando oyó eso.

51. Enseguida entendió el rey lo que decía.

52. Entonces dijo: —¿Dónde está ella?

53. *ʔį:^HR*   *ma^Lʔmá:ʔ^L =n*
look^here hid   I

54. *gó?^L =n ua^Mrá?^M gá^Lhŋë̃:?^L =? hnã̌^M*
afraid I   when   would^kill you me

55. *hą^L sá^L gá^Lhmé:^H =n hu:^H kʸá^H =? čá?^M*
then not report I   word to   you immediately

56. *hą^L ga^M gá^Lmí^Lhnä:^L <mozo> ?ẽ^M za^Lmẽ^M kʸá:^H gá^Lhę̃:^H*
then more showed   hired^man that woman his   to^see

    <rei>
    king

57. *gá^L?ę:?^L ba^M <rei>*
accepted (EMP) king

58. *gá^Ltő̃^H bí?^H*
released he

59. *hme:^M ba^M ?ne^L ta^M hnä^LR =n*
will^do (EMP) you work of   us

53. "I hid her.

54. I was afraid you would kill me.

55. Thus I didn't report it to you immediately."

56. Finally the hired man showed his wife for the king to see.

57. The king accepted it.

58. He abandoned (the matter).

59. "You keep doing my work.

53. —La escondí.

54. Tenía miedo de que me mataras.

55. Por eso no te lo informé inmediatamente.

56. Finalmente, el empleado le mostró su esposa al rey.

57. El rey lo aceptó.

58. Olvidó (el asunto).

59. —Tú sigue haciendo mi trabajo.

60. *mó^L tó^L*   *hme:^L* *ka^L lá?^M* *ba^M*   *há?^M* <*rei*>
    no^longer do   again   (EMP) said   king

61. *gá^L zá:^H* *hu:^H* *kí?^H*   <*rei*> *kʸą:?^M* <*mozo*> *kʸą́:^H*
    ended   story about king   and   hired^man his

60. Just don't do it again," said   60. Solamente no vuelvas a
    the king.   hacerme eso —dijo el rey.

61. The story of the king and the   61. Y así termina el cuento del
    hired man is finished.   rey y su empleado.

About a Rabbit who Buys a Guitar

1. *kǫ꞉^{L} ʔä^M ma^{M}ŋę̌^{L}*   *hą꞉^{L} lo^{L}k^{y}a^H tä̧꞉^{L} ku꞉ʔ^L*   *=i*
   once time used^to^walk a   rabbit white was^eating he

   ia^{L}mo꞉ʔ^L
   grass

2. *he꞉^{M} ŋę̌^{L} =i hą^L gá^{L}hę̌꞉^{H} =i hmé꞉^{L} hi꞉ʔ^H he꞉^{H} ia^{L}mo꞉ʔ^L*
   (LOC) walk he there saw   he make shiny (LOC) grass

   hą^L
   (PAUSE)

3. *ʔéʔ^H gá^{L}kǫ꞉^{H} =i*
   and took   he

4. *gá^{L}no꞉^{L} =i*
   stood   he

1. Once there was a white rabbit going around eating grass.

2. Where he was going along he saw something shining in the grass.

3. So he took it.

4. He stood up.

1. Había una vez un conejo blanco que andaba comiendo zacate.

2. Cuando él andaba caminando, vio algo brillante entre el zacate.

3. Así que, lo tomó.

4. Se paró.

5. $gá^Lhé:^H = i$
   looked   he

6. $h\varrho^L$ $l\acute{\varrho}:^M$ $= i$ $če^M$ $l\acute{\varrho}^L$ la^L ba^M $lá^H$ $ku:^M$
   then thought he ?   like this (EMP) is   money

7. $ku:^M$ $h\varrho^L$ $l\acute{\varrho}:^M$ $= i$
   money that thought he

8. $tá?^H$ $= i$ <$h^wërte$> $ma^Mgá^Llí?^H$ $= i$ $ku:^M$
   proud he strong   when^gained he money

9. $ní^L$ $k\varrho:^L$ $?e^L$ $lá^H$ $l\acute{\varrho}^L$ $h\varrho^L$ $sá^L$ $ma^Llï?^{MR}$ $= i$ $h\mu:?^H$ $hmï:^M$
   not one thing is like that not had^gained he while day

   $\eta\acute{e}^L$ $= i$
   walk he

10. $h\varrho^L$ $gá^Lhmé:^M$ $= i$ $?ü:^Mz\ddot{e}^L$ $?e^L$ $lá^H$ $= i$
    then did   he think   what will^buy he

5. He looked at it.

6. Then he thought, "Is this indeed what money is like?"

7. He thought it was money.

8. He was really tickled having
   found some money.

9. Not one thing had he ever got-
   ten like this as long as he had
   lived.

10. Then he thought about what
    he would buy.

5. Lo miró.

6. Entonces pensó: "¿Será así
   como se ve el dinero?"

7. Él pensó que era dinero.

8. Estaba encantado cuando
   encontró el dinero.

9. Nunca había tenido él una
   cosa así en toda su vida.

10. Entonces, él se puso a pensar
    en lo que compraría.

11. $ʔéʔ^H$ $lá:^M$ $=i$ $čér^M$ $gá^Llá^H$ $=n$ $ʔe^Mñi:ʔ^{HR}$ $čáʔ^M$ ba^M
    and think he if buy I bread immediately (EMP)

$žá^L$
will^run^out

12. $<i>$ $čér^M$ $gá^Llá^H$ $=n$ $<dulce>$ $lá^L$ ha^L $čáʔ^M$ ba^M
    and if bought I candy like that immediately (EMP)

$žá^L$ $ʔe^L$ ha^L $ka^Llá^{ʔM}$
will^run^out that that also

13. $<mejor>$ la^{HR} $=n$ $ko:^L$ tu^L
    better will^buy I a guitar

14. $lé^M$ ga^M $hme:^{LR}$ $=n$ $hmï:^M$ $k^ya:ʔ^M$ $ʔe^L$ ha^L
    will^be^possible more will^have I party with that (PAUSE)

$lá:^M$ $lo^Lk^ya^H$ $tä:^L$
think rabbit white

15. ha^L $gá^Llá^H$ $=i$ tu^L ba^M
    then bought he guitar (EMP)

16. $ʔéʔ^H$ $gá^Lʔno:ʔ^L$ $=i$ $ko:^L$ $he:^M$ $žú^H$ $gá^Lg^ya^L$ $=i$
    and looked^for he a place good sat he

11. He thought, "If I buy bread, it will indeed be gone right away.

12. And if I buy candy, likewise, it will indeed be gone right away.

13. It is better to buy a guitar.

14. Then I could have a party with it," thought the white rabbit.

15. So a guitar he did buy.

16. He looked for a good place to sit.

11. Él pensó: "Si compro pan, en seguida se me va a acabar.

12. Y si compro dulce, también se me irá en seguida.

13. Mejor compro una guitarra.

14. Entonces podría tener una fiesta con ella", pensó el conejo blanco.

15. Así que, compró una guitarra.

16. Buscó un buen lugar para sentarse.

17. *gá^{L}ʔíʔ^H* =*i* *tǫ^L*   *kíʔ^H* =*i*
    played he guitar of   him

18. *ma^{M}gá^{L}ʔíʔ^H* =*i* *tǫ^L*   *kíʔ^H* =*i* *ʔéʔ^H gá^{L}g^{y}a^L* =*i*
    when^played he guitar of   him and sat   he

19. *gá^{L}më́$\cdot^H$* =*i* *tï$\cdot^M$* =*i* *gá^{L}ló$\cdot^H$* =*i* *sá^H*   =*i* *tǫ^L*
    crossed he foot his began he played he guitar

20. *hlą$\cdot^H$* <*h^{w}ërte*> *iá^{L}ʔí$\cdot^H$*   *kǫ$\cdot^L$ sǫ^{HR} ʔe^L gá^{L}že^L* =*i* *k^{y}ą$\cdot^M$*
    good strong   came^out a   song that made he with

    tǫ^L   *kíʔ^H* =*i*
    guitar of   him

21. *gá^{L}tíʔ$^{H\wedge}$*<*h^{w}ërte*> *^zë́^{H}* =*i*
    really^liked   he

22. <*i*> *gá^{L}tíʔ$^{H\wedge}$*<*h^{w}ërte*> *^zë́^{H} h^{y}á^M há^M*   *ʔį$\cdot^L$ gá^{L}nú$\cdot^M$ sǫ^{HR}*
    and really^liked   other animals who heard song

    hą^L
    that

17. And he played his guitar.

18. When he played his guitar, he sat down.

19. He crossed his legs and he began to play his guitar.

20. It was a very pretty tune that he made with his guitar.

21. He really liked it.

22. And it really pleased other animals that heard the song.

17. Y tocó su guitarra.

18. Cuando estaba tocando su guitarra, se sentó.

19. Cruzó las piernas, y comenzó a tocar su guitarra.

20. Era una melodía muy bonita la que él tocó en la guitarra.

21. Le gustó de veras.

22. Y de veras le gustó a los otros animales que lo oyeron.

23. *má^{L}mi:ʔ^L lá^L h$ạ^L$ ba^M iá^{L}nä́:^{H} háʔ^M ʔ$ị$:^{L} gá^{L}nú:^{M}*
little^by^little like that (EMP) came animal who heard

lä́^{L}h$ị$:ʔ^H gá^{L}žá^{L}nä́:^{H} =i č$ụ$ʔ^L
until arrived they near

24. *to^{L}në^M gá^{L}žó:^{H} <liebre>*
first arrived jackrabbit

25. *<i> gá^{L}žó:^{H} h$ạ$:^{L} t$ạ$:^{H} č$ẹ$:^{L} <gorrión>*
and arrived a bird called sparrow

26. *<i> gá^{L}žó:^{H} hme^M*
and arrived skunk

27. *gá^{L}žá^{L}nä́:^{H} =i nu:^{L} =i ʔa^L lá^L hmé:^{L} lo^{L}k^{y}a^H t$ạ$:^{L} hmï:^{M}*
arrived they listen they how like make rabbit white party

k^y$ạ$:ʔ^M t$ụ^L$ kíʔ^H
with guitar his

28. *č$ạ$ʔ^M ba^M gá^{L}ŋí:^{M} hme^M t$ụ^L$ kíʔ^H lo^{L}k^{y}a^H*
immediately (EMP) asked^for skunk guitar of rabbit

---

23. Little by little animals who heard (the song) arrived until they had come up very close.

23. Poquito a poco los animales que oían (el canto) llegaban hasta que quedaron muy cerca de él.

24. A jackrabbit arrived first.

24. Una liebre llegó primero.

25. And then a bird called sparrow arrived.

25. Y después, llegó un pájaro llamado gorrión.

26. Then a skunk arrived.

26. Entonces llegó un zorrillo.

27. They arrived listening how the white rabbit made merry with his guitar.

27. Ellos llegaron a escuchar cómo el conejo blanco se alegraba con su guitarra.

28. Right away the skunk asked for the rabbit's guitar.

28. Inmediatamente, el zorrillo le pidió la guitarra al conejo.

29. *sá^L gá^Llá^Lbé^M^zé̱^H* =*i ko̠:^L gá^Lhé̱:^H* =*i tu̠^L*
    not could^endure he just was^looking he guitar

30. *ha̠^L gá^Lŋí:^M* =*i tu̠^L kíʔ^H lo^Lk^ya^H sá^H* =*i ko^Lʔ^wé̱:^M*
    then asked^for he guitar of rabbit played he little^while

31. *ha̠^L gá^Lhá̠ʔ^M hme^M k^wé̱:ʔ^{LR}* =*ʔ hná̱^M tú̠^M k^yá^H* =*ʔ*
    then said skunk give you me guitar of you

32. *sa^{HR}* =*n ko^Lʔ^wé̱:^M ami^{HR} há̠ʔ^M* =*i sí̠:ʔ^L* =*i lo^Lk^ya^H*
    will^play I little^while friend said he told he rabbit

33. *ná^H ka^Lhü:ʔ^L ŋë̠:^M* =*n k^yá^H* =*ʔ ka^Llá̠ʔ^M há̠ʔ^M hme^M*
    now shortly will^hand^over I to you again said skunk

34. *ha̠^L gá^Lhá̠ʔ^M lo^Lk^ya^H go^{HR} sá^L k^wa^{LR}* =*n ua^Mrá̠ʔ^M*
    then said rabbit likely not will^give I when

    gá^Ltí̠ʔ^H^h^wë̱rte^ʔó^M =*ʔ*
    really^like you

29. He couldn't stand it just look-
    ing at the guitar.

30. So he asked for the rabbit's
    guitar to play a little while.

31. Then the skunk said, "Give
    me your guitar.

32. I will play it for a little while,
    friend," he said to the rabbit.

33. "I'll give it right back to you,"
    the skunk said.

34. Then the rabbit said, "It is not
    likely I will give it lest you real-
    ly like it.

29. Él no podía aguantar estar
    sólo viendo la guitarra.

30. Así que, le pidió la guitarra al
    conejo para tocar por un ratito.

31. Entonces dijo el zorrillo:
    —Dame tu guitarra.

32. La tocaré por un ratito, amigo
    —le dijo al conejo.

33. Te la devolveré enseguida
    —dijo el zorrillo.

34. Entonces el conejo dijo: —No
    hay la posibilidad de que te la
    dé, a no ser que de veras te
    guste.

35. $ma^L\eta\ddot{e}^{:M}$ $h\underset{\cdot}{a}^L$ $s\acute{a}^L$ $t\underset{\cdot}{u}^{:L}{}^{\wedge}\widehat{?}\acute{o}^M$ $=?$ $\eta\ddot{e}^{:M}$ $=?$ $k\acute{\underset{\cdot}{i}}^L$ $=n$
after^that (PAUSE) not find^courage you hand^over you to me

$ka^L l\acute{\underset{\cdot}{a}}?^M$
again

36. $m\acute{a}^L d\acute{a}^L$ $hu^{:H}$ $z\acute{o}^{:M}$ $k\acute{\underset{\cdot}{i}}?^H$ $za^L\tilde{n}\ddot{u}^{:?L}$ na^L $h^w\underset{\cdot}{\acute{e}}^{:?MR}$ $=n$ $?ne^L$
just word true of man (PAUSE) am^telling I you

$h\acute{\underset{\cdot}{a}}?^M$ hme^M
said skunk

37. $\eta\ddot{e}^{:M}$ ba^M $hn\acute{\underset{\cdot}{a}}^M$ $k^y\acute{a}^H$ $=?$ $ka^L l\acute{\underset{\cdot}{a}}?^M$ $h\acute{\underset{\cdot}{a}}?^M$ $=i$
hand^over (EMP) I to you again said he

38. $h\underset{\cdot}{a}^L$ ga^M $g\acute{a}^L t\underset{\cdot}{u}^{:L}{}^{\wedge}z\underset{\cdot}{\acute{e}}^H$ $lo^L k^y a^H$ $?\acute{e}^M$
then more found^courage rabbit that

39. $g\acute{a}^L k^w\underset{\cdot}{\acute{e}}?^H$ $=i$ hme^M $t\underset{\cdot}{u}^L$ $k\acute{\underset{\cdot}{i}}?^H$ $=i$
gave he skunk guitar of him

40. $ma^M g\acute{a}^L ?^y\acute{o}?^H$ hme^M $t\underset{\cdot}{u}^L$ $h\underset{\cdot}{a}^L$ $g\acute{a}^L g^y a^L$ $=i$ $g\acute{a}^L s\acute{a}^H$ $=i$
when^received skunk guitar that sat he played he

35. After that you won't find
courage to hand it over to me
again."

36. "I am telling you nothing but
the truth," said the skunk.

37. "I will indeed hand it over to
you again," he said.

38. So at last the rabbit found
courage.

39. He gave his guitar to the skunk.

40. When the skunk received the
guitar he sat and he played it.

35. Después, no te vas a querer
dármela de vuelta otra vez.

36. —No te estoy diciendo más
que la verdad —dijo el
zorrillo—.

37. Por supuesto que te la voy a
dar después —le dijo.

38. Así que, al fin, el conejo se
atrevió.

39. Le dio su guitarra al zorrillo.

40. Cuando el zorrillo recibió la
guitarra, se sentó y tocó.

41. *ma^{L}ʔmí:^{M} g^{y}á^H hme^M sa^{MR} = i tṳ^L hạ^L hạ^L gá^{L}ŋí:ʔ^H*
    good^while sit skunk play he guitar (PAUSE) then asked^for

   lo^{L}k^{y}a^H tṳ^L kíʔ^H
   rabbit guitar his

42. *kọ:^{HR} = n tṳ^L kí^L = n*
    will^take I   guitar of me

43. *ʔị:^{HR} hnä́^{M} ŋá:ʔ^H = n hä́ʔ^M = i*
    as^for me am^going^home I   said he

44. *hạ:ʔ^ʔạ:^{H} sá^L ŋ̈ë:^{M} = n*
    no   not am^handing^over I

45. *ga^{L}tạ:^{M} ma^{L}k^{w}ë:ʔ^{LR} = ʔ hnä́^{M} k^{y}á^H = ʔ hä́ʔ^M hme^M*
    once^and^for^all gave   you me of you said skunk

46. *<pero> gá^{L}ʔó:ʔ^H lo^{L}k^{y}a^H*
    but   cried   rabbit

41. The skunk had sat playing the guitar a good while when the rabbit asked for his guitar.

42. "I will take my guitar.

43. As for me I am going home," he said.

44. "Oh no, I am not handing it over.

45. You gave it to me once and for all," said the skunk.

46. My, how the rabbit cried.

41. Un buen rato pasó el zorrillo tocando la guitarra; entonces el conejo le pidió de vuelta su guitarra.

42. —Voy a coger mi guitarra.

43. Creo que yo ya me voy para mi casa —dijo.

44. —¡Ah!, no, no te la voy a dar.

45. Tú me la diste de una vez por todas —dijo el zorrillo.

46. ¡Ay, ay, ay!, ¡Cómo lloró el conejo!

47. *gá^{L}zá^H ?o:^{M} lu:^{M} =i gá^{L}lá̌^{L}gú?^{M} če^{MR} =i hmï:^{L} tu̧:^{L} mï^{H}në̈^{M}*
    all^over mouth face his got^wet   wipe he tears fall eyes

    =i
    his

48. *me:?^{L}^zë̈^{H} =i <h^{wë}erte> kí?^{H} tu̧^{L} kí?^{H} =i*
    sad   he strong   about guitar of him

49. *ha̧^{L} gá^{L}hǎ?^{M} hme^M čér^M hme:^{L} =? ga^M ?ne^L bí:^{H} ŋï:?^{M}*
    then said   skunk if   make you more you deal ask^back

    =? tu̧^{L} la^L má?^{H} hë̈:^{H} =? ?a^L^lǎ^L lá^H ?e^L =n
    you guitar this and will^see you how   is   that I

    ?u̧:^{M} ?ne^L ná^H ka^{L}hü:?^{L}
    will^spray you now shortly

50. *gá^{L}hñú^H =i ó:^{L} ga^M mi:?^{L}*
    moved^aside he there more little

---

47. His whole face and neck were wet from wiping the tears from his eyes.

Chinantec commonly juxtaposes two words of similar meaning or of close proximity as in *?o:* 'mouth' and *lu:=i* 'his throat' to represent a broader meaning, in this case, face and neck.

48. He was really sad about his guitar.

49. Then the skunk said, "If you keep making a big deal asking for this guitar you will see how it is that I will spray you right quickly."

50. He moved aside a little bit.

---

47. Toda su cara y cuello se le mojaron cuando se secaba las lágrimas que le caían de los ojos.

Los chinantecos generalmente yuxtaponen dos palabras de significado similar o estrechamente relacionadas, como 'boca' y 'su garganta' para dar un significado más amplio; en este caso 'cara y cuello'.

48. Estaba de veras triste por su guitarra.

49. Entonces el zorrillo dijo: —Si continúas haciendo tanto ruido pidiéndome la guitarra ya vas a ver que yo te voy a rociar rápidamente.

50. Se movió un poquito hacia un lado.

51. <pero> láᴴ rá?ᴹ gáᴸgʸaᴸ bí?ᴴ
but   is   just   sat   he

52. níᴸ   sáᴸ   gáᴸhë̇:ᴴ   =i   ?aᴸ^láᴸ   láᴴ   he:ᴹ   gáᴸgʸaᴸ   =i
even   not   see   he   how   was   (LOC)   sat   he

53. láᴸta̧:ᴹ   nëᴹ   gʷa:?ᴴ   mí?ᴴ   gáᴸgʸaᴸ   =i
right^on upon hill   ants   sat   he

54. <pero>   <sin>   <lástima>   gáᴸbä̧:?ᴴ   mí?ᴴ   taᴸ?mï:ᴸ   =i
but   without pity   covered   ants   bottom   his

55. <pero> gáᴸku:?ᴸ   mí?ᴴ   kí?ᴴ   =i
but   bit   ants   *   him

56. he:ᴹ   ha̧ᴸ   gáᴸkʷáᴹ^hʷë̈ᴴ   gáᴸtó?ᴹ tu̧ᴸ   ha̧ᴸ
(LOC) there gave^opportunity   fell   guitar (PAUSE)

57. kʸa̧:?ᴹ   ?eᴸ   ha̧ᴸ   gáᴸkʸú̧:ᴴ   =i
with   that (PAUSE) ran   he

51. But he just sat,

51. Pero sólo se sentó.

52. He did not even see how it was where he sat.

52. No vio, ni siquiera, cómo estaba el lugar en que se sentaba.

53. He had sat right on an ant hill.

53. Se había sentado exactamente encima de un hormiguero.

54. Mercilessly the ants covered his bottom.

54. Sin misericordia, las hormigas le cubrieron las asentaderas.

55. My, how the ants bit him!

55. ¡Ayayay! ¡Cómo lo picaron las hormigas!

56. There then, that (situation) allowed the guitar to fall.

56. Entonces, eso (situación) hizo que la guitarra se le cayera.

57. With that he ran.

57. Por eso él corrió.

58. *gá^{L}ʔmá̈^{M}* =*i* *ʔo·^{M}*   *në̈^{M}* =*i* *ko^{L}te^{MR}*
    hid   he mouth face his completely

59. *ʔnó̈·^{H}* <*h^{w}ërte*> *lo^{L}k^{y}a^H*
    liked strong   rabbit

60. *gá^{L}ko·^{H}* =*i* *tų^L*   *kíʔ^H* =*i*
    took   he guitar of   him

61. *gá^{L}g^{y}a^L* =*i*
    sat   he

62. *gá^{L}më̈·^{H}* =*i* *k^{y}e^M* =*i*
    crossed he legs his

63. *gá^{L}ʔíʔ^H* =*i* *žú^H* *tų^L*   *kíʔ^H* =*i*
    played he well guitar of   him

64. *gá^{L}hë̈·^{H}* =*i* *tá^L*   *gü·ʔ^H*
    looked he toward up

58. He hid his head completely.

59. The rabbit really liked that.

60. He took his guitar.

61. He sat down.

62. He crossed his legs.

63. He played his guitar well.

64. He looked up.

58. Él escondió la cabeza completamente.

59. Al conejo de veras le gustó mucho eso.

60. Tomó su guitarra.

61. Se sentó.

62. Él cruzó las piernas.

63. Tocó bien su guitarra.

64. Miró hacia arriba.

65. *gá^{L}lǒ:^{H} =i hmé:^{L} =i hmï:^{M} ka^{L}lá$^?$^{M} lá^L$^?$mé:^{M}*
    began   he was^making he party   again   anew

66. *lá^L la^L ba^M lá^H <cuento> kí$^?$^{H} lo^{L}k^{y}a^H*
    like this (EMP) is   story   about rabbit

65. He began once again to make   65. Una vez más comenzó a estar
    merry.   alegre.

66. That's how the story of the   66. Así es la historia del conejo.
    rabbit is.

The Opossum and the Coyote

1. kǫːᴸ ʔäᴹ hạːᴸ maᴸhúːᴹ gáᴸhẹːᴴ =i hạːᴸ <coyote> maᴹčẹ́ʔᴴ
   one time an opossum met he a coyote standing

   ʔüːᴹ   kǫːᴸ móʔᴹ
   base^of a   mountain

2. ʔeᴸ hmeːᴸ =ʔ čẹ́ʔᴴ =ʔ heːᴹ naᴸ amiᴴᴿ žụ́ːᴴ kʸạ́ːᴸ =n
   what do   you stand you (LOC) there friend good of   me

   hä̃́ʔᴹ maᴸhúːᴹ sǐːʔᴸ <coyote>
   said opossum tell coyote

1. Once an opossum met a coyote standing at the foot of a mountain.	1. Una vez, un tlacuache se encontró con un coyote que estaba parado al pie de una montaña.
2. "What are you doing standing there, my good friend?" said the opossum to the coyote.	2. —¿Qué estás haciendo allí parado, mi amigo? —dijo el tlacuache al coyote.

3. $?i:^{HR}$ $hná^M$ $čé?^H$ $=n$ $čọ:?^M$ $=n$ $mó?^M$ $čí?^H$
   as^for me   am^standing I   am^holding I   mountain standing

   la^L
   here

4. $?nó:^H$ $tó?^L$
   about^to will^fall

5. $če^M$ $sá^L$ $hme:^H$ $=?$ $bé^M$ $kí^L$ $=n$ $há?^M$ <coyote>
   ?   not will^do you help for me said coyote

6. $gá^Llá^Lkạ:^L\_zé^L$ $=n$ $há?^M$ $ma^Lhú:^M$
   wholeheartedly I   said   opossum

7. $họ:^M$ da^M $hạ^L$
   wait (DDM) (PAUSE)

8. $ŋó:^H$ $=n$ $na^M?nó:^H$ $=n$ $?e^L$ $ki:?^M$ $=n$
   am^going I   will^go^get I   that will^eat we

9. $he:^M$ la^L $čọ:?^H$ $=?$ $mó?^M$ la^L
   (LOC) here will^hold you mountain this

3. "As for me I am standing holding up the mountain standing
   here.

4. It's about to fall.

5. Won't you help me?" said the
   coyote.

6. "Wholeheartedly," said the opossum.

7. "Wait.

8. I am going to go get something for us to eat.

9. Hold up this mountain.

3. —¿Yo? Estoy parado aquí
   sosteniendo la montaña.

4. Está a punto de caerse.

5. ¿No me ayudas? —dijo el
   coyote.

6. —De todo corazón —dijo el
   tlacuache.

7. —Espera.

8. Yo voy a conseguir algo para
   que comamos.

9. Sostén esta montaña.

10. *túᴸiáᴸtǫ́ᴹ* *uaᴹráʔᴹ* *gáᴸtóʔᴹ* *nëᴹ* *kʸáᴴ* *= ʔ* *hǎʔᴹ* *<coyote>*
   be^careful lest   fell   upon *   you said   coyote

11. *gáᴸʔíʔᴴ* *<coyote>* *huːᴴ*
   said   coyote   goodbye

12. *<i>* *ŋóːᴴ* *=i*
   and   went he

13. *ʔmíːᴹ* *koᴸteᴹᴿ* *ŋóːᴴ*   *<coyote>*
   long^time very   was^gone coyote

14. *maᴸʔʷa̧ːᴹ* *maᴸhúːᴹ* *čę́ʔᴴ* *=i* *čǫːʔᴸ* *móʔᴹ*   *ha̧ᴸ*
   tired   opossum stand he hold mountain (PAUSE)

15. *ha̧ᴸ* *la̧ːᴹ* *=i* *töᴴᴿ*   *=n* *móʔᴹ*   *laᴸ*
   then thinks he will^release I   mountain this

   máᴸkéᴸ   *gáᴸtóʔᴹ*
   even^though fell

16. *kʸǫ́ʔᴸ* *=n* *<hʷërte>*
   hungry I   strong

10. Be careful lest it fall on you,"
   said the coyote.

10. Ten cuidado, porque se puede
   caer sobre ti, dijo el coyote.

11. The coyote said goodbye.

11. El coyote se despidió.

12. And he left.

12. Y se fue.

13. The coyote was gone for a
   good while.

13. El coyote no regresó por un
   tiempo largo.

14. The opossum got tired standing holding the mountain.

14. El tlacuache se cansó de estar
   parado sosteniendo la montaña.

15. He thought, "I'm going to let
   loose of this mountain (even
   though) it fall.

15. Él pensó: "Voy a soltar esta
   montaña, aunque se caiga.

16. I am very hungry.

16. Tengo mucha hambre.

17. $n\ddot{\imath}{:}^{LR}$ $=n$ $na^{M}k\acute{u}{:}?^{H}$ $=n$
    will^go I   will^go^eat I

18. $g\acute{a}^{L}t\acute{o}^{H}$ $=i$ $m\acute{o}?^{M}$ $h\d{a}^{L}$ $m\acute{a}?^{H}$ $g\acute{a}^{L}k^{y}\d{\acute{u}}{:}^{H}$ $=i$ $ko^{L}\check{c}i{:}?^{M}$
    turned^loose he   mountain that and   ran   he rapidly

19. $ma^{L}\check{c}\d{\acute{e}}?^{H}$ $=i$ $\d{\acute{u}}{:}^{M}$ $m\acute{a}?^{H}$ $g\acute{a}^{L}h\ddot{e}{:}^{H}$ $=i$ $l\d{\acute{a}}^{L}ma^{L}\check{c}\acute{\imath}?^{H}$ ba^{M}
    now^standing he   far and   saw   he still^standing (EMP)

    $m\acute{o}?^{M}$ $h\d{a}^{L}$
    mountain (PAUSE)

20. $s\acute{a}^{L}$ $\check{c}a^{L}$ $g\acute{a}^{L}t\acute{o}?^{M}$
    not was fell

21. $g\acute{a}^{L}l\d{\acute{a}}^{L}?n\acute{e}{:}^{L}$ $=i$ $<h^{w}\ddot{e}rte>$
    got^mad   he strong

22. $h\d{a}^{L}$ $l\d{\acute{a}}^{M}{:}$ $=i$ $na^{M}?n\ddot{a}{:}?^{L}$ $=n$ $<coyote>$ na^{L} $m\acute{a}?^{H}$ $h\eta\ddot{e}{:}?^{HR}$
    then thought he   go^look^for I   coyote   that and   will^kill

    $=n$
    I

17. I am going to go eat."   17. Voy a comer."

18. He let loose of the mountain   18. Soltó la montaña y corrió
    and ran quickly.   rápidamente.

19. Standing far off he saw that   19. Parado a los lejos vio que la
    the mountain was still standing   montaña estaba todavía en pie
    (as it was).   (como antes).

20. It didn't fall.   20. No se había caído.

21. He got very mad.   21. Se enojó mucho.

22. He thought, "I'm going to go   22. Pensó: "Voy a buscar a ese
    look for that coyote and kill   coyote y lo voy a matar,
    (him).

23. *máʔ^H   sá^L hú:^H   =i ka^Llǎʔ^M h^yóʔ^M   hmï:^M*
    so^that not will^lie he again   another day

24. *ʔéʔ^H ŋó:^H =i*
    and   left   he

25. *ma^Mgá^Lžó:^H ma^Lhú:^M he:^M číʔ^H ko̱:^L ʔma^L he:^M ha̱^L*
    when^arrived   opossum   place stands a   tree   (LOC) there

    gá^Lhȩ́:^H =i <coyote>
    saw   he coyote

26. *ha̱^L hǎʔ^M ma^Lhú:^M ʔne^L gá^Lmí^Lga^H =ʔ hnǎ^M*
    then said   opossum   you   deceived   you me

27. *h^wǐ:^M =ʔ hnǎ^M tóʔ^L   móʔ^M   ma^Mčéʔ^H   =ʔ*
    told   you me   will^fall mountain when^were^standing you

    ma^Mčo̱:ʔ^M   =ʔ
    when^were^holding   you

23. So then he will not lie again
    another day."

24. And he left.

25. When the opossum arrived
    where a tree stood, there he
    saw the coyote.

26. Then the opossum said, "You
    deceived me.

27. You told me the mountain
    would fall when you were
    standing there holding it.

23. para que otro día no vuelva a
    mentir."

24. Y se fue.

25. Cuando el tlacuache llegó
    donde estaba un árbol, vio al
    coyote allí.

26. Entonces dijo el tlacuache:
    —Me engañaste.

27. Tú me dijiste que la montaña
    se caería cuando tú estabas
    parado allí, sosteniéndola.

28. *he:ᴹ hạᴸ gáᴸčέʔᴸ =ʔ hnã̌ᴹ hʷáʔᴹ =ʔ gáᴸžáᴸʔnŏ̌:ᴹ =ʔ*
    (LOC) there stood you me said you went^to^get you

    máᴸʔạ̌:ᴸ
    lunch

29. *maᴹsáᴸgáᴸñéʔᴴ =ʔ hạᴸ gáᴸtóʔᴴ =n móʔᴹ hạᴸ*
    when^not^returned you (PAUSE) released I mountain that

30. *sáᴸ gáᴸtóʔᴹ móʔᴹ*
    not fell mountain

31. *ná̌ᴴ miᴹʔma:ʔᴹ =ʔ kíᴸ =n ná̌ᴴ*
    now will^pay you to me now

32. *hạᴸ gáᴸŋí:ᴹ <coyote> hạ̌ᴸ ʔéᴹ hnã̌ᴹ ʔéᴹ gáᴸmíᴸgạᴴ =n*
    then answered coyote not who I who deceived I

    ʔneᴸ
    you

28. You had me stand there (and) you said that you were going to get lunch.

29. When you didn't return I let loose of the mountain.

30. The mountain didn't fall.

31. Now you are going to pay for it."

32. The coyote answered, "It wasn't me who deceived you.

28. Tú me tuviste allí parado, (y) dijiste que tú ibas a conseguir comida.

29. Cuando no regresaste, solté la montaña.

30. La montaña no se cayó.

31. Ahora, vas a pagar por eso.

32. El coyote contestó: —No fui yo el que te engaño.

33. go^{HR} $hạ{:}^L$ $<coyote>$ $ma^L\eta\acute{e}^M$ $t\acute{a}^L$ na^L $ko^L\check{c}i{:}?^M$ ba^M
    likely another coyote walked toward there rapidly (EMP)

   $?\acute{e}^M$
   who

34. $t\acute{a}^L$ $hme{:}^L$ $?ne{:}^L$ $=?$
    don't are^doing angry you

35. $h\ddot{e}{:}^{LR}$ da^M $\tilde{n}a^L$ $ua^Mki{:}?^M$ $=n$ $<chirimoyas>$ ko^Lte^{MR}
    see (DDM) come let's^eat we custard^apples completely

36. $<pero>$ $s\acute{a}^L$ $l\acute{i}{:}?^L$ $=n$ $u\ddot{i}{:}^{HR}$ $=n$ $g\ddot{u}{:}?^H$ $h\acute{a}?^M$ $ma^Lh\acute{u}{:}^M$
    but not know^how I will^climb I up said opossum

37. $h^w\acute{a}^H$ $hn\ddot{a}^{LR}$ $=n$ $kọ{:}^L$ $m\ddot{i}{:}^H$
    throw to us a fruit

33. It's likely (it was) another coyote who went by there quickly.

34. Don't be angry.

35. Look, come, let's eat some custard apples."

   Chirimoya is a round or oval fruit with a scaly skin. The fruit has white pulp and black seeds. In the United States it is commonly called sugar apple or custard apple *(Annona squamosa)*.

36. "But I don't know how to climb up," said the opossum.

37. "Throw me a fruit."

   The first person plural pronoun is commonly used as a polite form for first singular.

33. Puede ser que (haya sido) otro coyote que pasó rápidamente por allá.

34. No estés enojado.

35. Mira. Ven. Vamos a comer algunas anonas.

36. —Pero, yo no sé cómo subirme —dijo el tlacuache—.

37. Tírame una fruta.

   Se usa comúnmente el pronombre plural de primera persona como la forma de respeto para la primera de singular.

38. *hạ^L　gá^{L}h^{w}ạ́^{H}　<coyote>　kọ:^{L}　mï:^{H}　ʔe^L　h^{wi}:^{L}*
    then threw　coyote　　　one fruit that ripe

39. *hmạ́^{M}　　<h^{w}ërte>　ʔe^{L}hạ^L　gá^{L}ku:ʔ^L　=i*
    delicious strong　　　thus　　ate　　　he

40. *<i>　kọ:^{L}　gá^{L}ku:ʔ^L　ʔñï:^{M}　　<coyote>*
    and　one ate　　　　himself coyote

41. *hmạ́^{M}　　<h^{w}ërte>　hạ́ʔ^M　ma^{L}hú:^{M}*
    delicious strong　　　said　opossum

42. *h^{w}ạ́^{H}　ga^M　h^{y}óʔ^M　kọ:^{L}　mï:^{H}　hnä^{LR}　=n　hạ́ʔ^M　ma^{L}hú:^{M}*
    throw more another a　　fruit of　　us　said　opossum

43. *hạ^L　gá^{L}h^{w}ạ́^{H}　<coyote>　kọ:^{L}　mï:^{H}　ʔe^L　ʔ^{w}e:ʔ^L*
    then threw　coyote　　　one fruit that hard

44. *ʔe^{L}hạ^L　gá^{L}g^{w}ẹ́:^{H}　=i*
    thus　　choked　he

38. So the coyote threw a ripe fruit.

39. It was very delicious and so he ate (it).

40. And the coyote ate one himself.

41. "Very delicious," said the opossum.

42. "Throw me down another one," said the opossum.

43. So the coyote threw down a fruit that was hard (still green).

44. And so he choked (on it).

38. Así que, el coyote le tiró una fruta madura.

39. Estaba deliciosa, y por eso se (la) comió.

40. Y el coyote comió una también.

41. —Muy sabrosa —dijo el tlacuache—.

42. Tírame otra —dijo el tlacuache.

43. Entonces el coyote le tiró una fruta que estaba dura (todavía verde).

44. Y se atragantó (con ella).

45. $ta^{M}ko^{L}h\underline{i}{:}^{?H}$ $\check{c}\acute{e}^{?H}$ $=i$ $\check{z}e^{L}$ $=i$ $?e^{L}$ $h\underline{a}^{L}$ $\eta\acute{a}{:}^{?H}$
while stand he will^remove he * that go^home

<coyote> $k\acute{i}^{?H}$ $ko^{L}\check{c}i{:}^{?M}$
coyote his rapidly

46. $h\underline{a}^{L}$ $k^{y}\acute{\underline{a}}{:}^{H}$ $ma^{L}h\acute{u}{:}^{M}$ $za^{L}k\acute{i}{:}^{H}$ $za^{L}b\acute{\underline{a}}{:}^{H}$ $?^{w}\acute{\underline{a}}^{H}$
then lay^down opossum rolling rolling^up ground

47. $h\underline{a}^{L}$ ga^{M} $i\acute{a}^{L}n\acute{a}{:}^{H}$ $m\acute{i}^{?H}$
then more came ants

48. $g\acute{a}^{L}\check{z}e^{L}$ <chirimoya> $ma^{M}na^{L}g^{w}\ddot{e}^{M}$ $lu{:}^{M}$ $ma^{L}h\acute{u}{:}^{M}$ $?\acute{e}^{M}$
removed custard^apple was^stuck throat opossum that

49. $h\underline{a}^{L}$ ga^{M} $g\acute{a}^{L}no{:}^{L}$ $ma^{L}h\acute{u}{:}^{M}$
then more stood opossum

50. $g\acute{a}^{L}\check{z}\acute{a}^{L}\check{z}\acute{e}^{H}$ $=i$ $ka{:}^{?LR}$ $k\acute{i}^{?H}$ <coyote> $ka^{L}l\acute{a}^{?M}$
followed he behind * coyote again

45. While he was standing there trying to remove it, the coyote quickly went on his (way).

46. The opossum was lying writhing on the ground.

47. Then some ants came.

48. They removed the custard apple stuck in the throat of the opossum.

49. Then the opossum stood up.

50. He went after the coyote again.

45. Mientras él estaba parado allí, tratando de sacarla, el coyote siguió rápidamente su (camino).

46. El tlacuache estaba tirado, retorciéndose, en la tierra.

47. Entonces vinieron unas hormigas.

48. Sacaron la anona que estaba trabada en la garganta del tlacuache.

49. Entonces el tlacuache se paró.

50. Y fue detrás del coyote otra vez.

51. *gá^Lhę:^H* =*i ka^Llą́ʔ^M* <*coyote*> *čęʔ^H* =*i ku:ʔ^L* =*i*
   met   he again   coyote   stand he eat he

   <*tuna*>
   prickly^pear^fruit

52. *ʔne:^L* <*h^wërte*> *ma^Lhú:^M gá^Lhą́ʔ^M* =*i ʔe^Lla^H gá^Lh^wą́^H* =*ʔ*
   angry strong   opossum said   he why   threw   you

   <*chirimoya*> *sį́ʔ^M*
   custard^apple green

53. *hą́^L ʔé^M hną̈^M hą́ʔ^M* <*coyote*> *ʔé^M ka^Llą́ʔ^M*
   not that I   said coyote   that again

54. *lą́^Lhá^H   ba^M   hnä̈^M he:^M la^L*
   just^came (EMP) I   LOC here

55. *hë:^LR da^M   tá^L hme:^L ʔne:^L* =*ʔ*
   see (DDM) no   do   angry you

56. <*mejor*> *ña^L   ua^Mki:ʔ^M* =*n* <*tuna*>
   better   come let's^eat we prickly^pear^fruit

51. He met the coyote again, standing and eating prickly pear fruit.

52. Being very angry the opossum said, "Why did you throw a green custard apple?"

53. "That wasn't me," the coyote said again.

54. "Indeed, I just got here.

55. Look, don't be angry.

56. Better, just come and let's eat prickly pear fruit."

51. Se encontró con el coyote otra vez, parado y comiendo tunas.

52. Como estaba muy enojado, el tlacuache dijo: —¿Por qué me tiraste una anona verde?

53. —No fui yo —el coyote dijo otra vez—.

54. De veras, acabo de llegar aquí.

55. Mira, no estés enojado.

56. Mejor ven, y vamos a comer tunas.

57. *ha̧^{L} há̧$ʔ^M$ ma^{L}hú:^{M}* \<pero\> *sá^L lí:ʔ^L* =n *uï:^{HR}* =n
 then said opossum but not know^how I will^climb I

 gü:ʔ^H
 up

58. *h^{w}á̧^{H} kí^L* =n *ko̧:^{L} mï:^{H}*
 throw to me a fruit

59. *ha̧^{L} gá^{L}h^{w}á̧^{H}* \<coyote\> *ko̧:^{L} mï:^{H} ʔe^L na^{L}ʔ^{w}ï:ʔ^M ʔe^L sá^L*
 then threw coyote a fruit that was^peeled that not

 čo:^{H} tó̧:^{M}
 had thorns

60. *ma^{L}ŋȩ́:^{M} ha̧^{L} gá^{L}há̧ʔ^M* =i *ka^{L}lá̧ʔ^M h^{w}ä̧^{HR}* =n
 after^that (PAUSE) said he again will^throw I

 h^{y}ó̧ʔ^M ka^{L}lá̧ʔ^M
 another^one again

61. *ha̧:^{M} ʔo:^{M}* =ʔ *máʔ^H ku:ʔ^H* =ʔ *há̧ʔ^M* =i *sï:ʔ^L* =i *ma^{L}hú:^{M}*
 open mouth your and will^eat you said he told he opossum

62. *ha̧^{L} gá^{L}h^{w}á̧^{H}* \<coyote\> *ko̧:^{L} mï:^{H} lá̧^{L}k^{y}ȩ^{L} tó̧:^{M}*
 then threw coyote one fruit along^with thorns

57. So the opossum said, "I don't know how to climb up.

58. Throw me a fruit."

59. So the coyote threw a peeled fruit which had no thorns.

60. After that he said again, "I'm going to throw another one.

61. Open your mouth and eat (it)," he said to the opossum.

62. So the coyote threw a fruit, thorns and all.

57. Entonces, el tlacuache dijo: —No sé cómo subirme.

58. Tírame una fruta.

59. Así que, el coyote le tiró una fruta que no tenía espinas.

60. Después, dijo otra vez: —Voy a tirar otra.

61. Abre tu boca y cómela —le dijo al tlacuache.

62. Entonces el coyote le tiró una fruta con todo y espinas.

63. <i> gá^Lk^yǘ:^H =i
   and   ran   he

64. hạ^L za^Lbạ́:^H ma^Lhú:^M na^Lg^wë^{MR} <tuna>   lu:^M hị:^{?H}
   then roll^up opossum was^stuck prickly^pear^fruit throat until

   gá^Lžá^Lnạ́:^H mí^{?H} ?ị:^L gá^Lže^L   <tuna> hạ^L
   arrived   ants who removed fruit   that

65. ma^Mgá^Llá^H   ?e^L hạ^L ?é^{?H} gá^Lno:^L ma^Lhú:^M ŋó:^H =i
   when^had^happened *   that and stood opossum left he

   ko^Lči:^{?M}
   rapidly

66. ?na:^{?L}   =i <coyote> lạ́^Lhị:^{?H}   mó^Lsó^L   gá^Lhnạ́:^{?L}   =i
   look^for he coyote   until^now no^longer encountered he

   ko^Lte^{MR}
   completely

67. gá^Lzặ:^H hu:^H kí^{?H} ma^Lhú:^M k^yạ:^{?M} <coyote>
   ran^out story of   opossum and   coyote

---

63. And he ran.

64. So the opossum was rolling around (with) the fruit stuck in his throat, until the ants arrived and removed the prickly pear fruit.

65. After that, the opossum stood up and left quickly.

66. He looked for the coyote (whom) he never encountered at all.

67. That's the end of the story of the opossum and the coyote.

63. Y corrió.

64. Así que, el tlacuache estaba revolcándose (con) la fruta trabada en su garganta, hasta que llegaron las hormigas y le sacaron la tuna.

65. Después de eso, el tlacuache se paró y se fue rápidamente.

66. Buscó al coyote (a quien) nunca jamás encontró.

67. Así termina la historia del tlacuache y el coyote.

About Beings who Live in the River

1. *ko^Lžạ:^M za^L   há͏́ʔ^M lá͏́^L la^L*
   some   people say   like this

2. *hmé:^L =i   zo:^M hu:^H g^wạ:^H ʔe^L nu:^L =i*
   make they true story old   that hear they

3. *sá^L ʔnő:^H =i   za^Lʔạ:^LM za^Lzá͏̨^LM či:ʔ^L   ča^Mhmï:^L ua^Mráʔ^M*
   not want they fly   jump   children stream   when

   gá^Lžá^Lná͏̊:^H =i   žá^Llő:ʔ^H =i
   arrived   they go^bathe they

4. *čạ:^L ko^Lžạ:^M či:ʔ^L   za^Ltạ:ʔ^LR =i në^M kụ:^M*
   are some   children go^stand they upon rock

1. Some people say things like this.

2. They believe the old tales that they hear.

3. They don't want the kids to fly and jump into the water when they go to bathe.

4. There are some kids who go stand on the rocks.

1. Algunas personas hablan así.

2. Ellos creen los cuentos antiguos que oyen.

3. No quieren que los niños vuelen y se tiren al agua cuando se van a bañar.

4. Algunos niños se van a parar en las rocas.

5. *máʔ^H ʔlį:^L =i ča^Mhmï:^L*
   and   jump they water

6. *hą^L hå̂ʔ^M za^L g^wa̱:^H za^Lčų̌^M za^Lhő:^M k^ya:ʔ^M uį̂:^M kíʔ^H*
   then say people old will^shatter will^break bowl dish of

   za^L čą̱:^L ča^Mhmï:^L hå̂ʔ^M za^L
   people live water   say people

7. *ko̱:^L ʔä̱^M hą:^L či:ʔ^L čę́ʔ^H ką:ʔ^MR ʔmo:ʔ^L ča^Mʔo:^M hmï:^L*
   one time one child stand will^catch fish   edge   river

   ta^Mko̱^Lhį̱:ʔ^H čę́ʔ^H čo:^H =i ʔnä̱^MR k^wį̱:^LR ʔe^L kǫ́:^L =i
   while   stand mother his cut   firewood that will^carry she

8. *zą́:ʔ^H =i há^H =i iá^Llő:ʔ^L =i*
   go^home she came she came^bathe she

9. *gá^Lhę́:^H či:ʔ^L ʔé̱^M gá^Ltą:ʔ^LR ʔmo:ʔ^L né̱ʔ^L ko̱:^L mï^Hkų̱:^M mä:ʔ^L*
   saw   child that entered fish   under one rock   small

   k^ye:^L ča^Mhmï:^L
   lie water

---

5. And they jump into the water.

6. The old people say, "The dishes of the people who live in the water will be broken to bits," people say.

7. Once a kid was trying to catch fish at the edge of the river, while his mother was cutting firewood to carry home.

8. She was on her way home having come to bathe.

9. The kid saw some fish had entered under a little rock lying in the water.

---

5. Y brincan dentro del agua.

6. Los viejos dicen que los platos de la gente que vive en el agua se van a hacer pedacitos, dice la gente.

7. Una vez un niño estaba cogiendo peces a la orilla del río mientras su mamá estaba cortando leña que iba a llevar a la casa.

8. Ella se iba a la casa, porque había venido a bañarse.

9. El niño vio unos peces que se metieron bajo una roca que estaba en el agua.

10. *haˡ gáˡká̧ᴴ =i ko̧:ˡ mïᴴku̧:ᴹ ʔeˡ ko̧:ˡ ó̧:ʔˡ =i čó:ᴴ*
then carried he one rock that one managed he will^raise

=i
he

11. *máʔᴴ naᴹno̧:ˡ =i nëᴹ ku̧:ᴹ he:ᴹ ñí:ᴹ*
and stood he upon rock (LOC) high

12. *gáˡhʷá̧ᴴ =i ku̧:ᴹ ha̧ˡ nëᴹ ku̧:ᴹ he:ᴹ gáˡta̧:ʔᴸᴿ ʔmo:ʔˡ ʔéᴹ*
threw he rock that upon rock where were fish those

13. *he:ᴹ ŋó:ᴴ =i hë:ᴸᴿ =i čeᴹ maˡhú̧:ᴴ ʔmo:ʔˡ ʔéᴹ gáˡhȩ́:ᴴ =i*
(LOC) went he look he if died fish those saw he

iáˡʔȩ́:ᴴ ha̧:ˡ zaˡ čaᴹhmï:ˡ
came^out one person water

14. *ko̧:ˡ ʔnaᴴ bíʔᴴ lá̧:ᴴ =i zaˡ*
one half him is he person

15. *ko̧:ˡ ʔnaᴴ =i lá̧:ᴴ =i háʔᴹ ča̧:ˡ čaᴹhmï:ˡ*
one half him is he animal lives water

10. So he took (as big) a rock as he could manage to raise.

10. Así que, tomó una piedra (las más grande) que él podía levantar.

11. And he went to stand on a rock where it is high.

11. Y fue a pararse a lo alto de una roca.

12. He threw the rock on top of the rock where the fish were.

12. Tiró la piedra sobre la roca debajo de la cual estaban los peces.

13. As he went to see if the fish had died, he saw a person come out of the water.

13. Cuando fue a ver si se habían muerto los peces, él vio a una persona salir del agua.

14. Half of him was a person.

14. Una mitad de él era una persona.

15. One half of him was like a water animal.

15. Y la otra mitad de él era como un animal acuático.

16. ha^L $gá^Lhá?^M$ za^L $?é^M$ $sí:?^L$ $=i$ $či:?^L$ $?é^M$ $lá^L$ la^L $?ne^L$
    then   said   person   that   tell   he   child   that   like   this   you

     ba^M na^L $té:^L$ $=?$ ta^M na^L $h^wá^M$ $=?$ $ku:^M$ $he:^M$
     (EMP)   (PAUSE)   good^at   you   work   there   throw   you   rock   (LOC)

     la^L $kí^L$ $=n$
     here   of   me

17. $má?^H$ $za^Lhó:^M$ $lá^Lhě^L$ $he:^M$ $hmé:^L$ $=n$ $?e^L$ $kú:?^L$ $=n$
    and   will^break   all   (LOC)   make   I   what   will^eat   I

18. $za^Lhó:^M$ $?^ya^L$ $kí^L$ $=n$
    will^break   pots   of   me

19. $za^Lhó:^M$ $u\underset{\sim}{í}:^M$ $kí^L$ $=n$
    will^break   dish   of   me

20. <pero> $gá^Lh^wa:?^H$ $či:?^L$ $?é^M$ $ma^Mgá^L?lé:?^M$ za^L $?é^M$
    but   were^frightened   child   that   when^spoke   person   that

     $lá^L$ ha^L
     like   that

16. So the person said, he told the kid like this, "So you are the one who is good at throwing rocks at my place.

17. And everything with which I make my food will break.

18. My pots will break.

19. My dishes will break."

20. The kid was really frightened when the person spoke like that.

16. Entonces, la persona dijo, le dijo al niño: —Así que tú eres el que es bueno para tirar piedras a mi casa.

17. Todas las cosas en que hago la comida (lo que uso para hacer comida) se van a quebrar.

18. Mis ollas se van a quebrar.

19. Mis platos se van a quebrar.

20. El niño se asustó de veras cuando la persona le habló así.

21. *gá^{L}të·^{L} =i čo·^{H} =i ma·^{LR} hä́ʔ^M =i*
    called he mother his mother said he

22. *ʔe^L hä́ʔ^M čo·^{H} =i*
    what said mother his

23. *ko^{L}či·ʔ^M ñeʔ^{HR} =ʔ ia^{L}hë·^{LR} da^M ko·^{L} ʔi·^{L} za^L la^L*
    rapidly come^back you come^see (DDM) one who person this

    hä́ʔ^M =i
    said he

24. *ʔéʔ^H háʔ^H čo·^{H} =i ko^{L}či·ʔ^M*
    and came^back mother his rapidly

25. *ha$_i$^{L} gá^{L}háʔ^M za^L ʔé^M sí·ʔ^L =i za^{L}mé̜^{M} ʔé^M za^{L}mé̜^{M} hä́ʔ^M*
    then said person that told he woman that woman said

    =i če^M mi^{M}ʔma·ʔ^M =ʔ ʔe^L ʔl̈i·ʔ^H ma^{L}hmé·^{M} či·ʔ^L k^{y}ä̜·^{H} =ʔ
    he ? will^pay you what damage did child of you

    la^L hä́ʔ^M =i
    this said he

21. He called his mother:
    "Mother," he said.

22. "What?" said his mother.

23. "Quickly come see once who
    this person is," he said.

24. And his mother came back
    quickly.

25. Then the man said to the
    woman, "Woman," he said,
    "Will you pay for the damage
    your kid did?" he said.

21. Él llamó a su mamá:
    —¡Mamá! —dijo a su mamá.

22. —¿Qué? —dijo su mamá.

23. —Ven rápido a ver quién es
    esta persona —le dijo.

24. Y su mamá vino rápidamente.

25. Entonces el hombre le dijo a
    la mujer: —Señora —le dijo
    —, ¿Pagará ud. el daño que su
    hijo hizo? —le dijo—.

26. $<o>$ $če^M$ $mi^L?ma:?^{LR}$ $=i$ $?ñí:^M$ $=i$ $hå?^M$ za^L $?é^M$
    or   ?   will^pay   he himself he said person that

27. ha^L $gá^Lhå?^M$ $za^Lmě^M$ $?é^M$ $?e^L$ $ma^Lhmé:^M$ $gü:^L$ $k^yá:^L$ $=n$
    then said   woman that what did   baby of   me

28. $ma^Lhmé:^M$ $=i$ $?ña:^L$_$zě^H$ $=i$
    did   he mean   he

29. $ma^Lhö:^H$ $=i$ $k^ya:?^M$ $uí:^M$ $kí^L$ $=n$
    broke   he bowl dish of me

30. $mi^M?ma:?^{LR}$ $=n$
    will^pay   I

31. $?a^L$ $lå^L$ $ko:^H$ $=?$ $hå?^M$ $za^Lmě^M$ $?é^M$
    how^much like will^take you said woman that

32. $ŋë:^M$ $=?$ $ha:^L$ $gü:^L$ $ča:?^M$ $hå?^M$ za^L $?é^M$
    hand^over you a   baby chicken said person that

26. "Or will he pay for it himself?" he said.

27. The woman said, "What did
my baby do?"

28. "He was mean.

29. He broke my pots and pans."

30. "I will pay.

31. How much will you take?"
said the woman.

32. "Hand over a baby chicken,"
said the man.

26. ¿O lo pagará él mismo? —dijo
él.

27. La señora dijo: —¿Qué hizo
mi niño?

28. —Él es necio.

29. Él quebró mis ollas y cazuelas.

30. —Yo pagaré.

31. ¿Cuánto le debo? —dijo la
mujer.

32. —Déme un pollito —dijo el
hombre.

33. *na^L   ma^L?í:^M   gá^Lá̰:?^H   =i*
    then right^then disappeared he

34. *ko̰:^L   ma^Lžá?^H baM   za^Lmê^M ?é^M maMgá^Lhnő:?^H   ha̰:^L gü:^L*
    once arrived (EMP) woman that when^she^found one baby

    kʸá̰:^H =i zo:^M tá̰^Mbé^M
    of   her sick rapidly

35. *<i> gá^Lhṵ́:^H =i*
    and died   he

36. *he:^M   ha̰^L   gá^Lzá̰:^H <cuento> za^L   ga:^H ?ê^M*
    (LOC) there ended story   people old that

33. Right then he disappeared.

34. No sooner did the woman arrive home than she found one of her babies sick all of a sudden.

35. And he died.

36. There ends the story of the old people.

33. En ese instante desapareció.

34. Tan pronto como la mujer llegó a su casa uno de sus niños se enfermó repentinamente.

35. Y se murió.

36. Así termina la historia de la gente antigua.

Publications in the
Language Data Amerindian Series

1. **The Cuiva language grammar** by Marie Berg and Isabel Kerr. 1973. 105 pp. *Microfiche only.*
2. **The grammar of Tunebo** by Paul Headland. 1973. 76 pp. *Microfiche only.*
3. **Southern Barasano grammar** by Richard D. Smith. 1973. 75 pp. *Microfiche only.*
4. **Cayuvava texts** by Harold Key. 1974. 75 pp. *Microfiche only.*
5. **Lexicon-dictionary of Cayuvava-English** by Harold H. Key. 1975. 201 pp. *Microfiche only.*
6. **A syntactic study of Tlingit** by Constance M. Naish. 1979. 176 pp. *Microfiche only.*
7. **A morphological study of Tlingit** by Gillian L. Story. 1979. 214 pp. *Microfiche only.*
8. **Sayula Popoluca verb derivation** by Lawrence Clark. 1983. 180 pp.
9. **From phonology to discourse: Studies in six Colombian languages,** ed. by Ruth M. Brend. 1985. 133 pp.
10. **Workpapers concerning Waorani discourse features,** ed. by Evelyn G. Pike and Rachel Saint. 1988. 168 pp.
11. **Ozumazín Chinantec texts,** compiled by James E. Rupp and Nadine Rupp. 1994. 96 pp.
12. **Mitla Zapotec texts,** compiled by Morris Stubblefield and Carol Stubblefield. 1994. 152 pp.

For further information or a catalog of SIL publications write to:

International Academic Bookstore
Summer Institute of Linguistics
7500 W. Camp Wisdom Road
Dallas, TX 75236

www.ingramcontent.com/pod-product-compliance
Lightning Source LLC
Chambersburg PA
CBHW050540270326
41926CB00015B/3316